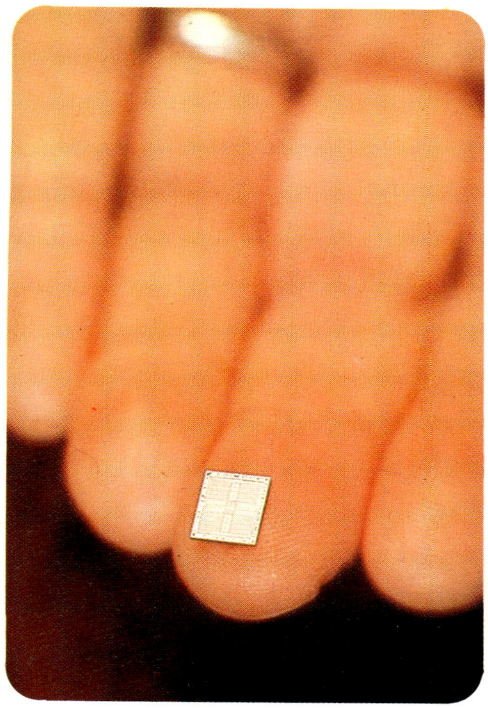

FOREWORD

The subject of computers is approached with a variety of feeling: excitement, awe, fascination, intimidation. In business, industry and scientific research the computer is an essential tool and as time goes by they have an increasingly intimate place in everybody's lives: in the home, in schools and at work.

Have you ever wanted to know more about these electronic machines? Well, read on . . .

This book deals in a straightforward way with the many aspects of the computer: an outline of the history; a description of the parts; an introduction to how they work and a study of the many and varied applications to which they are put. Computer jargon is explained and there are many photographs and illustrations providing an interesting introduction to computers for children and their parents.

Acknowledgements

Photographs kindly supplied by Acorn Computer Ltd; Apple Computers (UK) Limited; Control Data Ltd; The Controller of Her Majesty's Stationery Office; Epson (UK) Ltd; N. Filipek; Halifax Building Society; International Computers Ltd; National Westminster Bank PLC; Philips Business Systems Ltd; Plessey Semiconductors Ltd; Science Museum; Science Photo Library (James Bell, Martin Dohrn, Charles Falco, Tom McHugh, Jerry Mason/New Scientist, Ohio Nuclear Corporation, David Parker, P. Ryan, H. Scheebeli, Science Source, Don Thompson, John Walsh); Servis; Sinclair Research Ltd; Software Sciences Ltd; I. M. Spence; D. W. Thorley; Walt Disney Productions Ltd. 'Colour Genie' on front cover courtesy of Lowe Computers, Matlock.

Contents

What are Computers?	6
How Computers Developed	7
Parts of a Computer	11
Putting Information into the Computer	13
The Central Processing Unit	16
Memory	17
Receiving the Results	20
The Silicon Chip	22
Telling a Computer What to Do	25
How Computers Work	29
Computers Everywhere	33
Here to Stay	44
Computer Dictionary	45

Published in Great Britain by
World International Publishing Limited
P.O. Box 111, Great Ducie Street, Manchester M60 3BL.
Printed in Italy.
SBN 7235 7046 9.

Let me tell you about...

COMPUTERS

by David W. Thorley and Nina Filipek

WHAT ARE COMPUTERS?

A computer can take many different forms. One computer will send out electricity bills while another will control a spaceship. You can play an exciting game on a small computer or use large computers to forecast the weather. There are millions of computers in the world and they can cost from under a hundred pounds to millions of pounds.

So what is a computer? Put simply, a computer is an electronic machine which does things to information it is given and supplies us with the results. What it does to information, it does according to instructions given, which it can store for use again and again. Computers can work with information very rapidly, carrying out millions of instructions a second and they can be made to hold vast quantities of information. However, they can only do what they are instructed to do.

All computers have many basic ideas in common and we hope that when you have read this book you will have an understanding of what the world of computers is all about.

Computers come in many shapes and sizes.

A desk top computer

A business computer

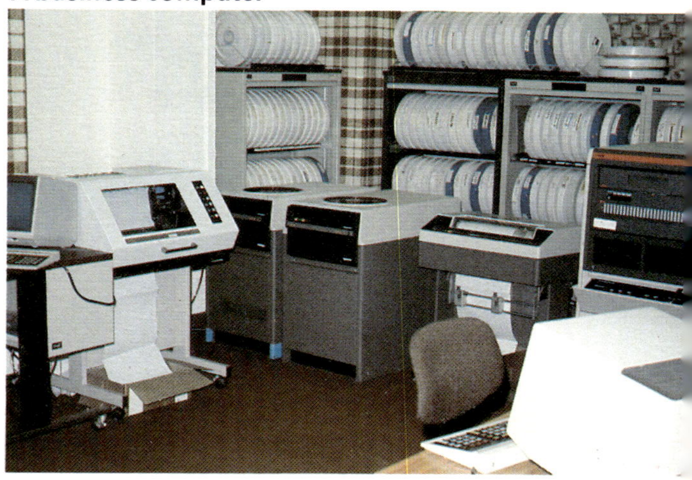

A computer to play tunes on

A toy to help you spell

Part of a computer that handles cash

A computer you can use anywhere

HOW COMPUTERS DEVELOPED

From Early Ideas . . .

Throughout history man has constantly looked for ways of making calculations easier. In the ancient world the abacus, or counting frame, was commonly used. Beads or stones were threaded onto a number of rods held in a frame. The first rod represented units, the second tens, the third hundreds and so on. Calculations were done by moving the beads along the wires. In parts of Asia the abacus is still used even today and expert users can obtain answers to calculations as quickly as with a pocket calculator.

Chinese Abacus

An important development in the history of computers was the invention of the slide rule in the early part of the seventeenth century. Numbers were represented on a special scale, known as a logarithmic scale, on two rulers, and the results of multiplications and divisions could be read by sliding the rulers next to each other.

In 1642 a Frenchman called Blaise Pascal invented the first mechanical calculator. Numbers were represented as teeth on a set of gear wheels. Numbers could be added or subtracted by simply turning the wheels.

Pascal's Calculating Machine

In 1821 Charles Babbage, an English mathematician, began to build the *Difference Engine* to calculate mathematical tables. Alas, the machine was never successfully completed because at the time it was just not possible to build it accurately enough. Despite this he went on to set out his ideas for what he called an *Analytical Engine.* This also was never built, but his ideas are important because he had designed the first automatic computer. It would have been possible to enter numbers and instructions and do complicated arithmetic, storing the results at each stage.

Part of Babbage's Analytical Engine

To Early Computers

The next major advance was made by Herman Hollerith, an American statistician who worked in the Bureau of the Census. It became apparent that the job of counting and sorting the return from the 1890 Census wouldn't be finished by 1900 when the next census was due! He saw that the answer lay in some measure of mechanisation using punched cards. He realised that answers such as "yes" or "no" could be represented by the presence or absence of a hole punched in the card and more complex information could be coded by using a group of holes.

A machine was developed which could read punched cards using electricity: a hole would allow electricity to pass through and the absence of a hole would stop it. In this way the cards were read, counted and sorted.

Hollerith's Sorting and Counting Machine

In the 1940s work began on the first electronic computers. In 1946 ENIAC (Electronic Numerical Integrator and Calculator) was built at the University of Pennsylvania. It took two years to build and used 18,000 valves. It was designed to work out the target distances of artillery used in World War II. The use of electronics enabled the operating speed to be increased enormously, ENIAC could do 5,000 calculations a second. However, ENIAC could not store information or instructions and for this reason the Manchester University Mark I, which first ran in June 1948, is considered to be one of the first true computers because it could store information and instructions.

Computers built in the 1940s and early 1950s were awesome in size and they were controlled by means of thousands of valves which used a great amount of power and which often overheated, thus they were costly to run and were subject to failure due to heat problems.

The Manchester University Mark I

. . . Then Rapid Progress

In 1948 three American scientists, Bardeen, Brattan and Shockley, invented a device which became known as a transistor. It could perform the functions of a valve but was smaller, cheaper, less fragile, more reliable, used less power and didn't get so hot. For these reasons transistors quickly began to replace valves in computers from 1953.

In 1958 an American named Jack Kilby discovered a way of putting more than one transistor onto a single piece of silicon. The transistors were linked together to make paths or circuits through which an electric current could pass. This was known at first as an *integrated circuit* but because it was made from a small piece of silicon it became known as the *silicon chip* or just *chip*.

The U.S. government – which was by now deeply involved in the space race and needed more powerful computers for their spacecraft – were immediately interested in this new development. In the 1960s the government sponsored research into integrated circuits at places such as the Santa Clara Valley in California, which became known as Silicon Valley. The silicon chip was to revolutionise electronics. Soon, a few chips could replace hundreds of transistors.

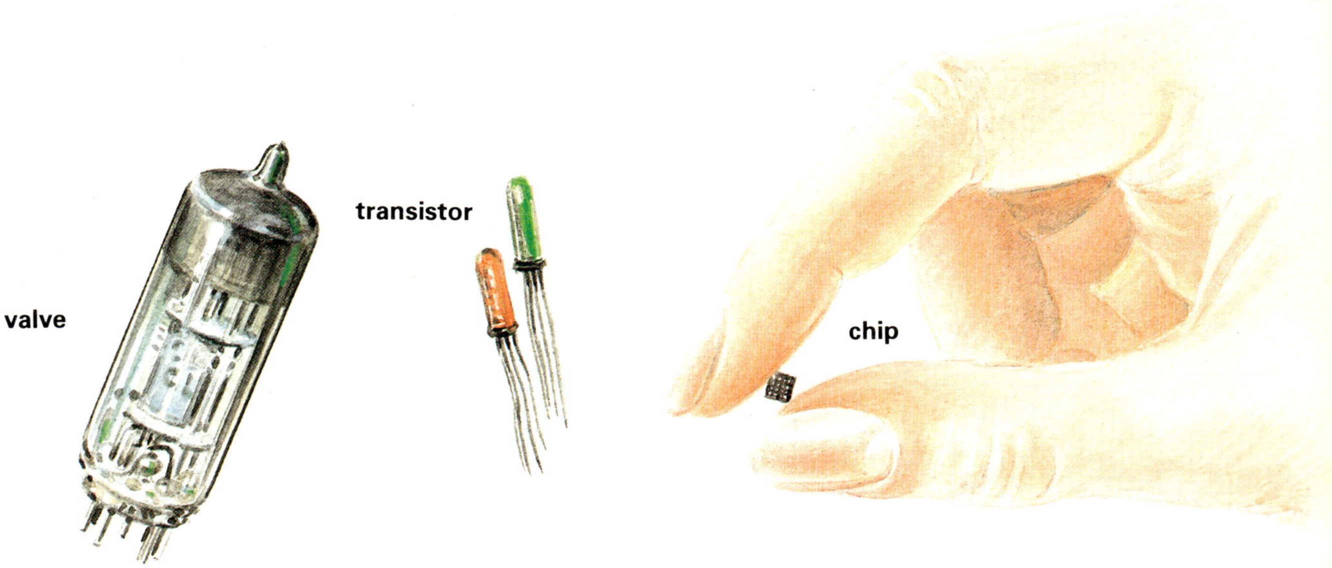

The complexity of the integrated circuit increased and more and more components were packed onto the same chip. Until in 1971 it was possible to put all the main electronic components of a computer onto a single chip called the microprocessor.

This brings us up to the present day when it is possible to build computers of enormous logical capacity and reliability more cheaply and in a very small space.

An integrated circuit magnified sixty-three times.

Today's Computers

Today we can say that there are three main types of computer, namely the mainframe computer, the minicomputer and the microcomputer.

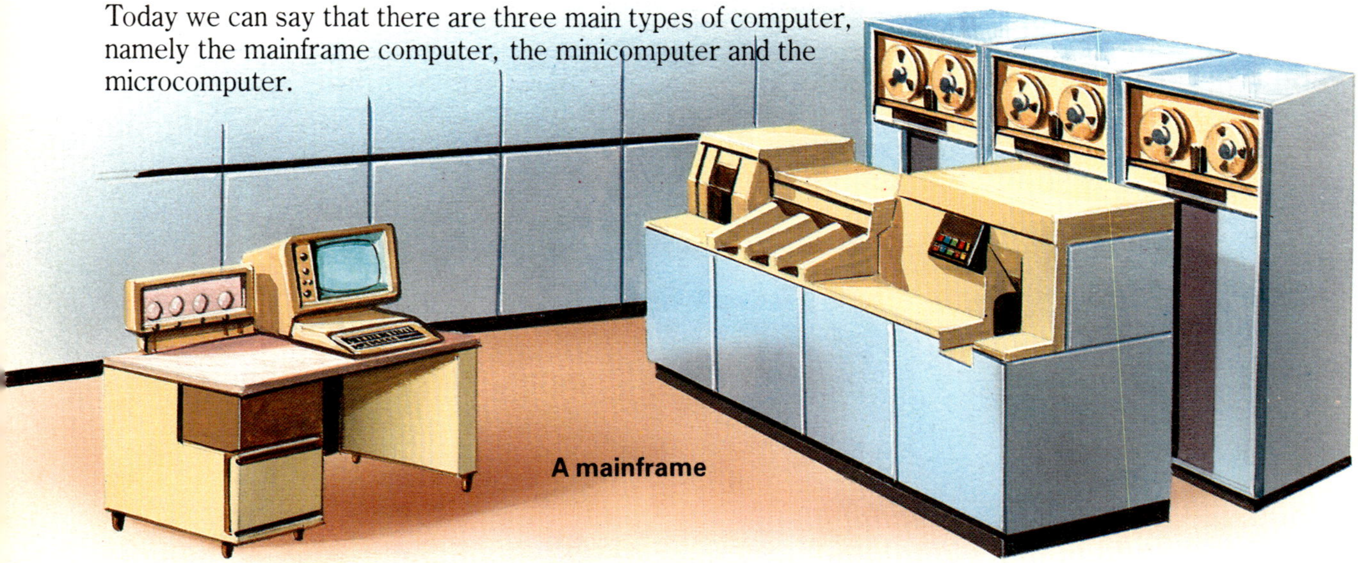

A mainframe

The mainframe is the largest and the most powerful of these. A mainframe installation contains rows of different units, some allow input of information to the computer, others display or store the results. A mainframe computer can handle vast amounts of information, it can carry out millions of instructions every second and it can do several different jobs at the same time. A really powerful computer such as this would be used in a very large company.

A minicomputer

A microcomputer

The minicomputer is not as big or as powerful as the mainframe and it is generally used for one particular job, such as accounting or storing information for a databank. Nevertheless, it is still much more powerful than the early computers built in the 1940s.

The smallest and the least powerful is the microcomputer. Microcomputers are mainly used in offices, homes and schools.

PARTS OF A COMPUTER

There are two elements which work together to make up a computer system: hardware and software.

These are the parts that make up the hardware of a mainframe computer.

The hardware is the name given to all the equipment and electronic circuits that make up the computer – the keyboard, screen, tape-recorder, disk drive, printer. However, the hardware can do nothing without the software.

There is a huge variety of programs available.

The software is the name given to the information that the computer needs to work on. The information can be instructions which tell the computer what to do, or data which is information that is used by the instructions. For example, you can instruct a computer to add two numbers together. The actual numbers that are entered into the computer for it to add are the data. A set of instructions that perform a task is known as a program. You cannot *'touch'* software but it can be stored on magnetic tapes, disks or punched cards.

The hardware of a computer system has four main parts or units, each unit is linked together as shown in the diagram. However, these units are quite separate in that each has its own special job to perform.

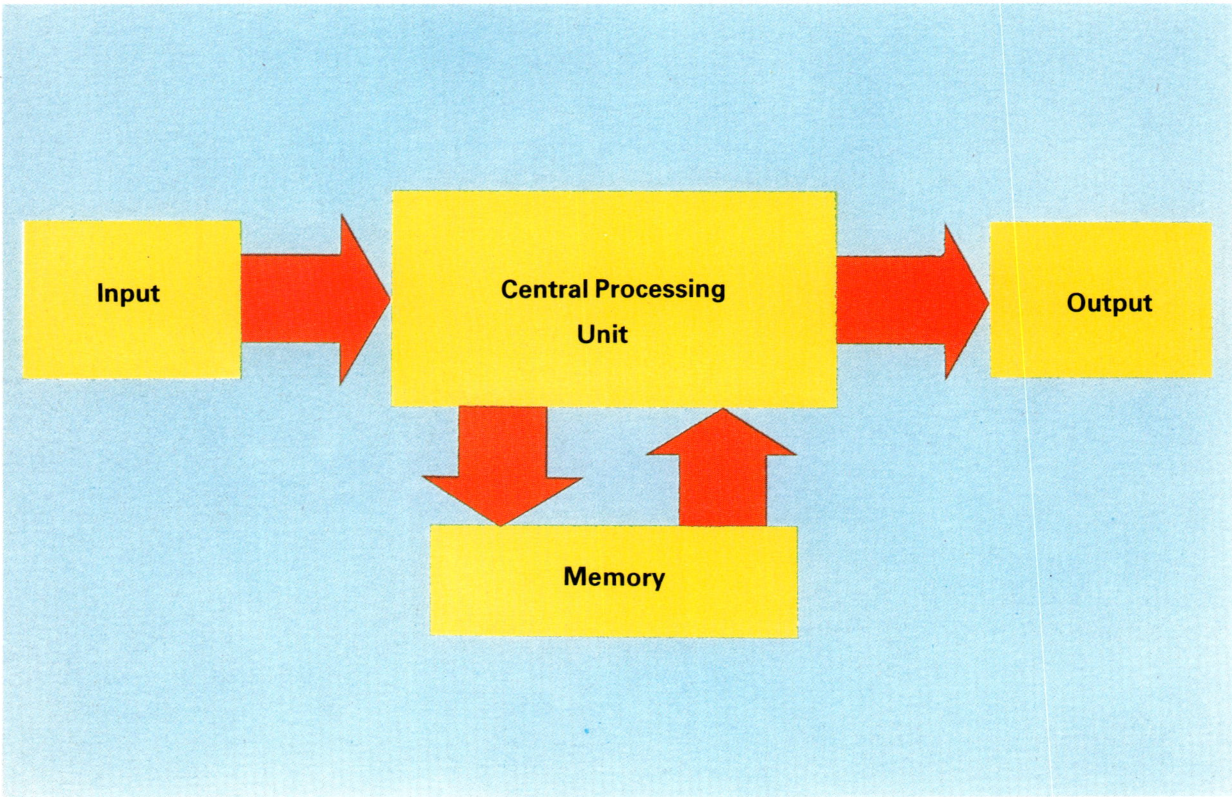

1. INPUT UNIT

The input unit is like the 'eyes' and 'ears' of the computer. Information is put into the computer from the outside world using the keyboard, joystick or other input equipment. The input unit turns the information into a series of electronic pulses which the computer can understand and passes it on to the Central Processing Unit.

2. CENTRAL PROCESSING UNIT (CPU)

It is here that the actual work is done. The CPU is like the 'brain' of the computer. It takes information from the input unit and from the memory and uses or processes it according to the instructions the computer has been given. It may put information into the memory or give results to the output unit.

3. MEMORY

The computer memory stores instructions and information that the computer is currently working on or that will be needed at a later time.

4. OUTPUT UNIT

The computer uses the output unit to give its results to the outside world. The electronic pulses passed from the CPU may be turned into something we can see printed or displayed on a screen, something we can hear or even something that will control other machines for us.

In the following pages we will firstly learn more about these hardware units and then something about software and finally some of the tasks computers are given to do.

PUTTING INFORMATION INTO THE COMPUTER

The keyboard

A computer cannot deal with information unless it is coded into a language it understands. So the input unit translates all information into electronic pulses that the computer can work with.

THROUGH THE KEYBOARD

To input information in the form of words and numbers, the most widely used device today is the keyboard.

Letter and number keys are arranged like those on a typewriter but there are also some extra keys and particular key combinations that help us give instructions to the computer.

Underneath the keys there is a grid of criss-crossing wires. When a key is pressed a metal contact touches a cross-point on the grid and each cross-point has a particular pattern of electronic pulses so that the computer knows which key has been pressed.

USING A JOYSTICK

In games like space-invaders, when you need to move spacecraft quickly across the screen the keyboard can be rather awkward; here, the joystick is easier to use and it enables greater control.

There are electrical contacts in the base of the joystick that translate every movement of the handle into an instruction for the processor.

The joystick is fun to use

WITH THE MOUSE!

The mouse is a similar device to the joystick. The joystick lever is replaced with a rolling ball and the unit is turned upside down. As the unit is rolled to and fro across the desk, instructions are sent to the processor to move a pointer on the screen in the same way.

The mouse

WITH THE GRAPHICS PAD

A graphics pad has a magnetically sensitive surface which allows shapes to be drawn or traced with an electronic pen. The pad is sensitive to the movements of the pen and it turns these movements into electronic pulses which the computer can process.

Similarly, the touch tablet has a touch sensitive pad which can be used as a graphics tablet to write or draw on the screen.

THROUGH SPEECH

It would be much easier for us if we could simply tell the computer what to do. However, input in the form of spoken instruction is the most difficult to handle and is still a major area of research. Teaching a computer to understand speech is a complex process. First the sound must be translated into electrical signals by a microphone and then into an electronic code that the computer can memorise. The computer is told what each code requires it to do such as 'stop' or 'go'. When somebody then speaks into the unit the electronic code is compared with those in memory and the computer can carry out the required action. Because people's voices vary so much, the computer has to remember the voices of each person who will be using it. All this takes up a great deal of the computer's memory.

Information in the form of drawings can be put into the computer by using a graphics pad.

A designer using a graphics pad to produce a drawing of an electronic circuit board.

BY ELECTRONIC READING

Magnetic character recognition (MCR) is used by banks to read numbers on cheques. With this system the figures are typed using magnetic ink and the input unit reads the magnetised shapes.

Although computers cannot read normal handwriting, optical character recognition (OCR) systems can read specially designed forms if letters are written separately in boxes and are carefully shaped. OCR units shine light onto characters and a camera picks up reflected light and the pattern is translated into electronic pulses.

In some supermarkets the check-out assistant uses a similar device to read the patterns of black stripes or bar codes that are printed on packages.

More details of these devices are given later in the book.

WITH OTHER INPUT UNITS

There are many other forms of input unit. Machines can be used to punch holes on cards or paper tape, which can then be used with an input unit which can read these holes. A light pen interacts with a screen and can be used to draw on a screen or alter a display. In science and industry input units may take the form of specialised measuring instruments or sensors; for example, a device may measure the temperature or weight in an industrial process and pass the measurements into a computer.

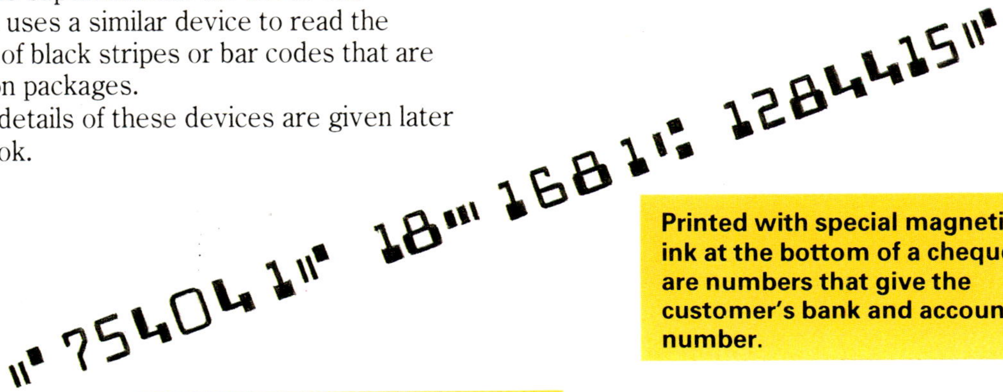

Printed with special magnetic ink at the bottom of a cheque are numbers that give the customer's bank and account number.

A bar code is a pattern of parallel lines of different thicknesses. The different thicknesses form a code number which is often also printed at one side of the pattern. Look at the bar code on the back of this book!

Using a light pen you can draw directly on the screen.

THE CENTRAL PROCESSING UNIT

The central processing unit (CPU) the brain of the computer, comes in many different sizes. The CPU of mainframes are like large cupboards and can carry out millions of arithmetic operations a second. The CPU of a microcomputer is much less powerful and is contained in a single chip. All CPUs work in a similar way using three main sections: the arithmetic and logic unit (ALU), registers and a control unit. The connections between the units which carry information in the form of electrical pulses are called buses. Let us now look in a bit more detail at the three main sections in a typical microcomputer CPU chip.

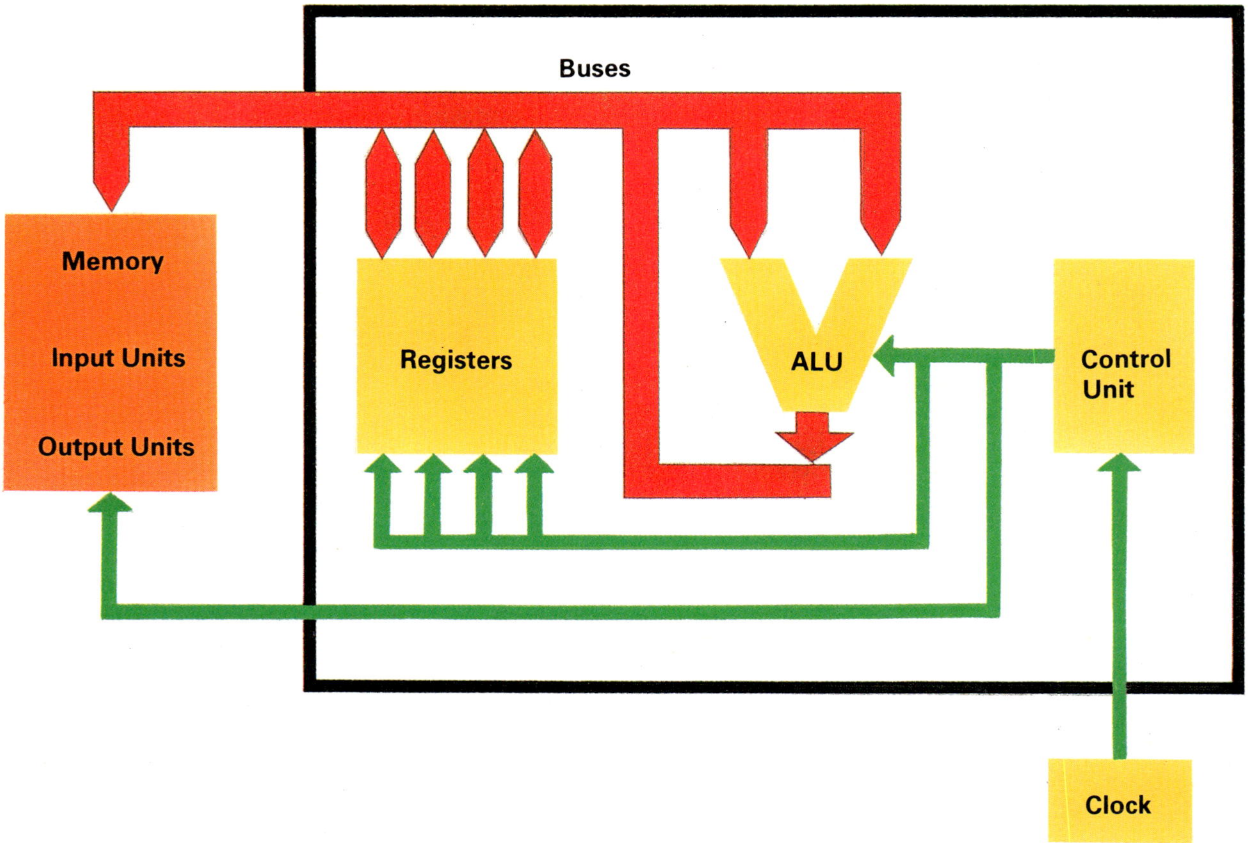

1. ARITHMETIC AND LOGIC UNIT

In the ALU, calculations such as adding two numbers together are carried out. The ALU can also carry out logical operations like comparing two numbers to see which is the larger. A modern computer can perform a single addition in nanoseconds (a nanosecond is a thousand millionth of a second!).

2. REGISTERS

The CPU has a small memory of its own. It is provided because it works extremely rapidly to store information about a particular problem the CPU is working on.

3. CONTROL UNIT

The control unit gets each instruction in turn and arranges for it to be carried out. The control unit may have to tell the ALU to perform a task or move information in or out of the registers. It can also get information from the input unit, send information to the output unit or transfer information to or from the computer's memory.

It is important that everything is done in exactly the right order and at the right time, so there is an accurate clock within the computer which is connected to the control unit.

MEMORY

Memory is required because the computer must be able to store information. The instructions in a program need to be stored so that they can be used again and again without having to enter them each time through the input unit. Similarly the data needs to be stored in order to be available when it is required.

There are basically two types of memory – internal memory or main store and external memory or backing store.

A circuit board showing rows of memory chips.

INTERNAL MEMORY

In a modern computer, internal memory is usually contained in silicon chips. It holds instructions and data which the computer is currently working on or information which the CPU needs before it can work at all. Internal memory needs to work very rapidly because the speed of the CPU is very high and requires information to be readily available. The more powerful the computer the more internal memory it will require. Memory chips are of two types: ROM and RAM.

1. ROM Chips

ROMs or Read Only Memories hold sets of instructions which tell the microprocessor what to do. For instance, a ROM will tell the processor how to recognise which key has been pressed and how to light up the screen.

A ROM never forgets. Information stored on a ROM can only be 'read', it cannot be rubbed out or added to.

2. RAM Chips

RAMs are designed to act as short-term memory. A RAM holds information which is needed for a particular operation. New information can be recorded, read and then rubbed out when no longer needed. But once the computer is switched off a RAM forgets everything.

RAM stands for Random Access Memory which means that the CPU can find each part of the memory straight away. This is similar to looking up a word in a dictionary. You can go straight to the word you want to look at, you don't have to start at the beginning and read through the book until you reach the word. The CPU can find each part of the memory because each part is numbered. This number is called the address of the memory location.

EXTERNAL MEMORY

A computer's internal memory is usually not large enough to hold all the information it needs and when a computer is switched off everything stored on RAMs disappears. But, information which is written in its external memory will stay there for ever and can be wiped off and the same area used to store new information.

Today tapes and disks are commonly used as external memory. Both work on the same principle: information is written onto a magnetic material by magnetising tiny areas on the surface in a form the computer can understand.

Mainframes use tape drives with reel to reel tape.

Tapes

Magnetic tape is a strip of plastic with a thin film of magnetic material on one side. Magnetic tape is fairly cheap but is slow to use because magnetic spots are laid down in rows along the length of the tape and so to find a particular piece of data, the computer must start at the beginning of the tape and read through until it reaches it.

Home microcomputers can use an ordinary cassette player and tape as an external memory, but computers in business need units which are faster, more reliable and can hold more information. These use large specially designed reel to reel tape recorders.

With most microcomputers you can use an ordinary cassette player and tape.

Disks

Similarly disks are made of a magnetically-coated material. The surface of each disk is marked with invisible circular tracks, and data is recorded as magnetic spots following these tracks. A disk drive is used to read and write the information on them. Data stored on a disk can be found much faster than with tape because the head of the drive which reads and writes magnetically can go immediately to the track on the disk where the required information is held. Disks and disk drives are much more expensive than tape and tape units.

Microcomputers usually use floppy or flexible disks which are made from flexible plastic. The disks are held in a cardboard cover to protect them, with a slot cut out to allow the head to read and write to the disk. The disk holding the information required is loaded into the disk drive.

Large computers use hard disks which hold more information and allow faster reading and writing. These are usually sealed in plastic cases and may be arranged in a pack of a few disks.

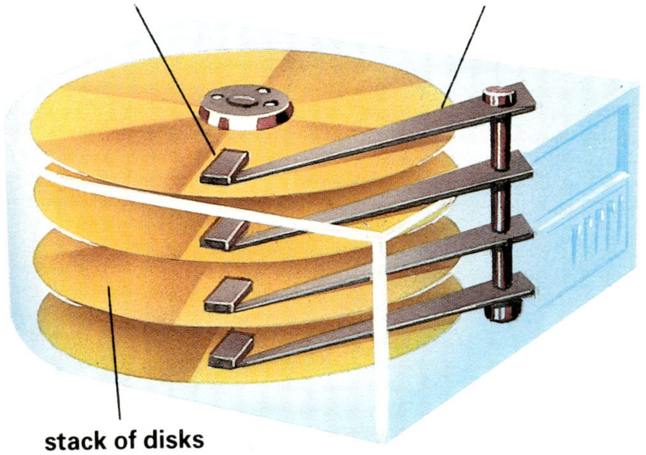

A separate head reads each disk.

A large system will use many disk drive units.

RECEIVING THE RESULTS

When the information has been processed by the CPU the output unit then translates the results back into a form we can understand.

ON THE SCREEN

Screens can display results in the form of numbers, words and pictures. Many smaller microcomputers use ordinary television screens, others have their own special screen, often called a Visual Display Unit or VDU. Screens can display detailed pictures in colour which are often called graphics. The pictures are made of many dots called pixels and can be used for games and displaying diagrams. The more pixels a screen is capable of displaying the more detailed a picture will be. In computing this is referred to as resolution, the more detailed the picture the higher the resolution.

The screen is often closely linked with the keyboard so that the characters that are typed in are immediately displayed, allowing the person who is keying in to check that he or she has entered the information correctly.

low

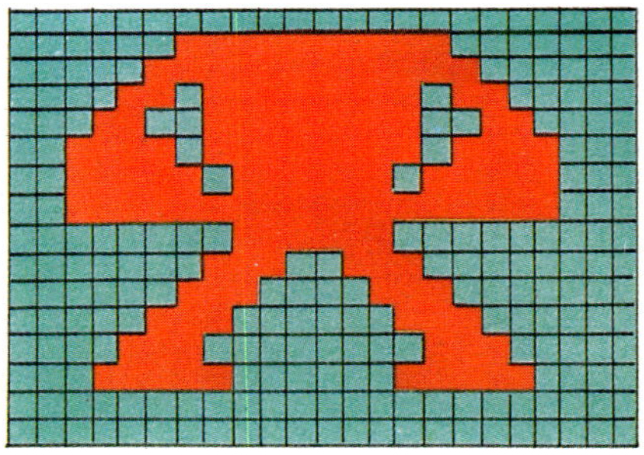

With low resolution there is a rougher edge, curves are difficult to draw.

high

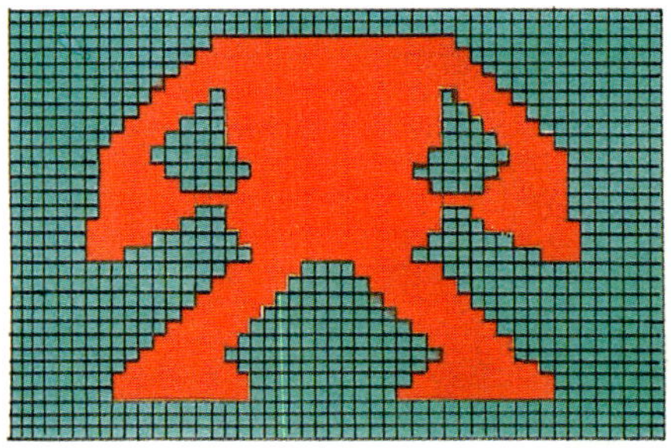

With high resolution finer lines can be drawn.

A dot matrix printer

This is how the dot matrix printer works.

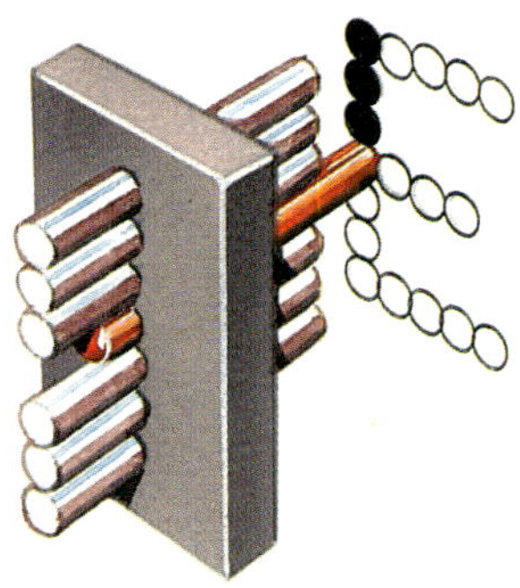

IN PRINTED FORM

The printer is used when a permanent record of results is needed.

The dot matrix printer forms numbers, letters and graphics from patterns of dots. It usually has seven needles arranged in a vertical line. Electronic pulses instruct the print head as to the correct pattern of dots which are fired onto a typewriter ribbon and then onto the paper as the print head moves across. This type of printer is very versatile and is most often used if the printing is wanted in the form of graphics.

The thermal printer is similar, except that here the image is formed by heating the required pattern of needles which burns the shape on heat sensitive paper.

Daisy wheel printers are designed for use with word processors. They can produce high quality text, in differing styles.

Letters and numbers are marked on the rim of a circular plastic disk. As the disk spins, a hammer hits the appropriate character against the ribbon and onto the paper.

The printers so far mentioned will usually print less than 100 characters a second when working with a micro. This is much faster than a typist, but larger computers require much faster printing speeds and so use much more complex printers. These printers will print whole lines at a time using a print device at each character position. They operate at up to 1,000 lines per minute!

A line printer

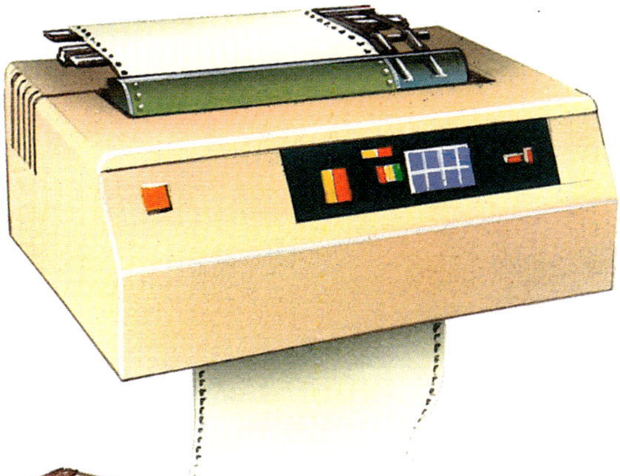

A daisy wheel printer works like this.

A plotter

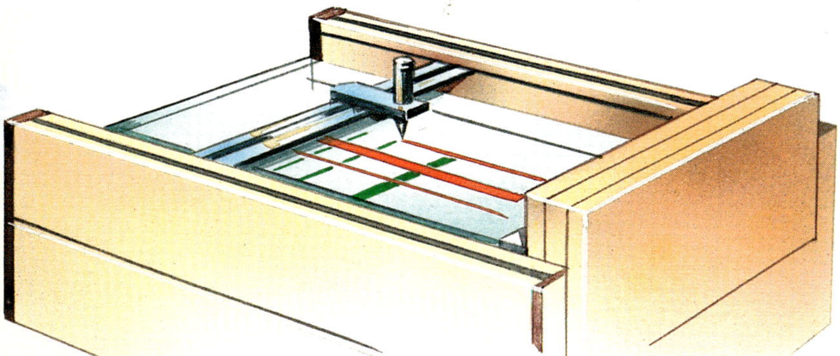

THROUGH A PLOTTER

Often used by designers and architects who require accurate drawings; a plotter can draw graphs, pictures or words. The plotter is guided across the paper by signals from the computer. Plotters may use several pens containing different coloured inks.

IN SOUND

If an output unit consists of a synthesizer the computer can produce sound. A synthesizer gives an electronic signal which when passed into a loudspeaker will produce a sound. The CPU can control the synthesizer to produce musical notes or even words which can be understood as human speech.

THROUGH OTHER OUTPUT UNITS

There are many other specialised output units.

Robotic arms which are used in car manufacturing are a type of output unit because they are controlled by electronic pulses from a computer. Traffic lights can be computer controlled and when you make a telephone call a computer will be involved in connecting your call.

THE SILICON CHIP

As we have seen, the greatest advances in the development of computers came with the invention in 1958 of the integrated circuit or 'chip'. Since then, scientists have constantly sought for ways of making chips more powerful by increasing the number of components on a smaller and smaller area, thus shortening the distance over which information has to be sent, so that the speed at which the computer works has increased. The result has been that today it is possible to pack more than a million components onto a piece of silicon which can pass through the eye of a needle, and this has meant that a modern computer can work at a speed measured in nanoseconds.

Silicon, the raw material from which chips are made, is very cheap and when made in huge numbers production costs are kept low.

Chips use very little power themselves and so they can run in battery powered devices such as watches, calculators, cameras and toys.

Finally, chips are reliable, having in-built wiring and no moving parts which can break or wear out; they are extremely robust.

Not surprisingly then, some have argued that the chip is the most important invention of this century!

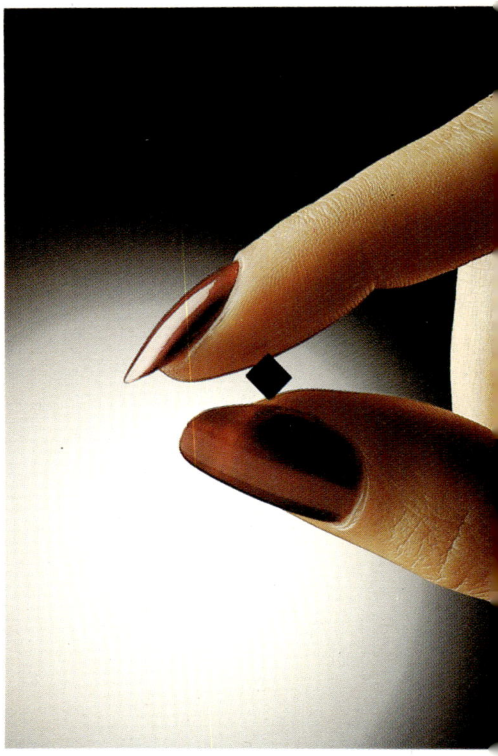

This microprocessor chip controls an automatic washing machine.

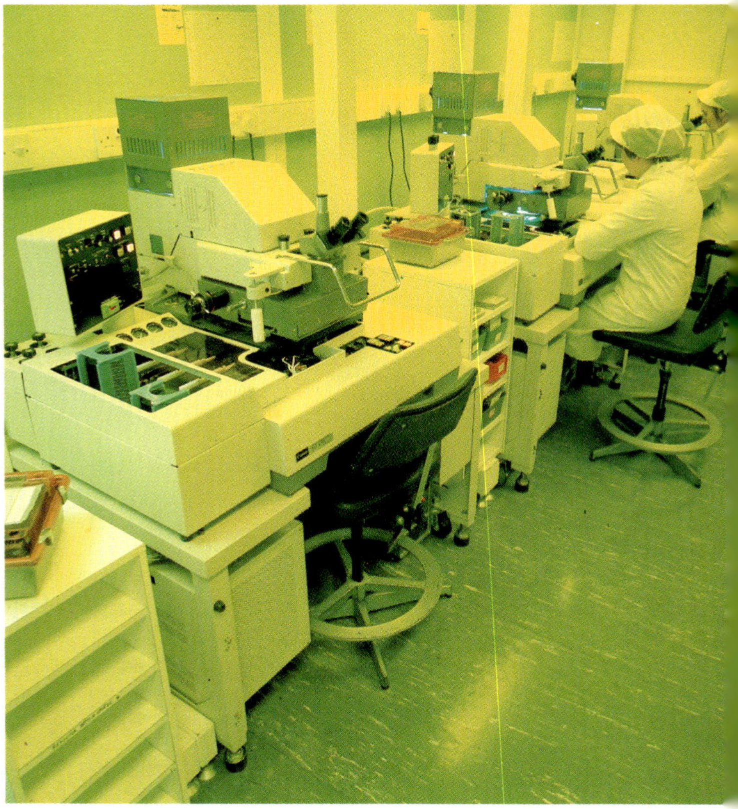

Workers in a dust free chip factory. The process of chip making is explained on the opposite page.

MAKING CHIPS!

At all stages of the manufacturing process absolute precision is essential. Not surprisingly perhaps, computers supervise and control production techniques. Factories, equipment and workers must be completely clean and dust-free; a single speck of dust could damage a whole circuit.

1)
The design stage is the most expensive and the most difficult part of the whole production process. Computers help in designing and testing circuits. On a single chip there can be as many as ten different circuits, each containing thousands of components, built up in layers of different chemicals on the surface of the silicon. However, once a circuit has been designed, providing large numbers of that particular design are manufactured, then production costs can be kept low.

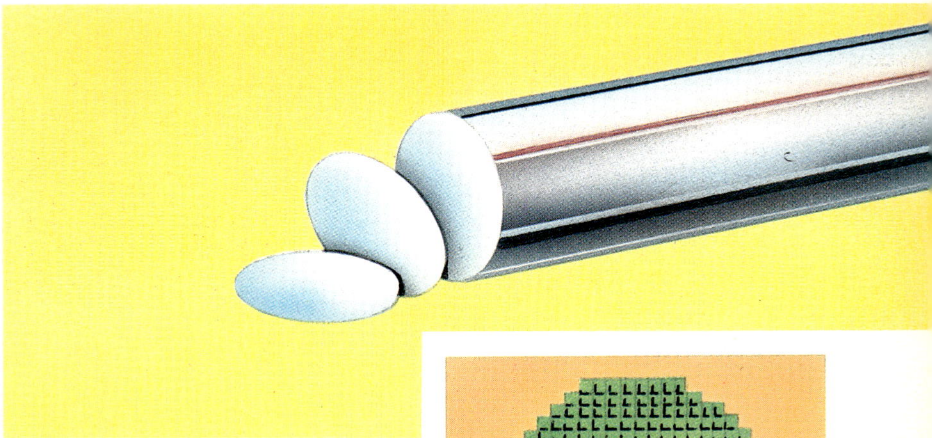

2)
A tiny silicon crystal is put into a vacuum oven containing pure melted silicon. As the liquid silicon cools the crystal grows until it is about one metre long. Then it is polished into a smooth cylinder shape and cut into round wafers about half a millimetre thick. The wafers are polished until mirror-smooth. Each wafer will make approximately five hundred chips.

3)
The circuit designs for each layer of the chip are photographically reduced in size and copied onto a set of 'photomasks'. A mask holds the tiny circuit designs all the same, side by side. Using a chemical process circuit images are then transferred onto each wafer of silicon.

4)
Every tiny circuit on the wafer is tested using electrical probes and a powerful microscope. At this stage as many as 70% of the five hundred or so are found to be faulty. Each wafer is cut into separate chips and those previously marked as faulty are discarded.

5)
After more tests the perfect chips are mounted on plastic cases with pin connectors so that they can be linked up to other units.

TYPES OF CHIP

There are many different types of chip used in a computer. Chips can have different circuits on them and so perform different functions. The CPU of a microcomputer is one sort of chip and is known as a microprocessor chip. Microprocessor chips are also used to control all kinds of equipment from cameras to robots. A sophisticated computer can have several microprocessor chips. ROM chips and RAM chips are used for the internal memory. Interface chips are also used in computers. These allow communication between the CPU and input units, output units and external memory, converting electrical pulses so that each unit understands the information that is being sent.

TELLING A COMPUTER WHAT TO DO

A computer doesn't have a brain like ours. It cannot do anything by itself but has to be told exactly what to do. The problem is that a computer cannot understand our language so when we want to tell it something we have to do so in a special computer language. We can give a command or instruction to a computer which is to be carried out straight away. We also need to be able to store a set of instructions which are to be carried out over and over again or at a later time.

A set of instructions written in the computer language is called a program. Writing a program is called programming and so the computer languages are called programming languages. A program can be stored on a tape or disk so that it is available to be run whenever we want.

PROGRAMMING LANGUAGE

In the computer everything is done using electronic pulses. There is a special program which translates your instructions into these electronic pulses that the computer can understand. This can be done because the instructions are written according to strict rules. For example, they contain special words and symbols and the order of the words is very important.

The pattern of electronic pulses which the processor can understand is called machine code. In fact we could write instructions in machine code but it is very difficult, so special programming languages have been developed. Even though they have to be written carefully they are much easier to understand and quicker to use than machine code.

THERE IS MORE THAN ONE LANGUAGE

There are many programming languages in use. The one most commonly used on microcomputers is BASIC. The letters stand for Beginners' All Purpose Symbolic Instruction Code.

PASCAL is sometimes used on small computers and many people think that it is better than BASIC. PASCAL is named after the French mathematician who invented the mechanical calculator.

On business computers the programming language COBOL is usually used. Here the letter stand for COmmon Business Orientated Language.

For scientific works ALGOL (ALGOrithmic Language) or FORTRAN (FORmula TRANslator) are often used.

In education the language LOGO has been designed to help children learn about programming.

This section of a COBOL program checks that a date has been entered into the computer correctly.

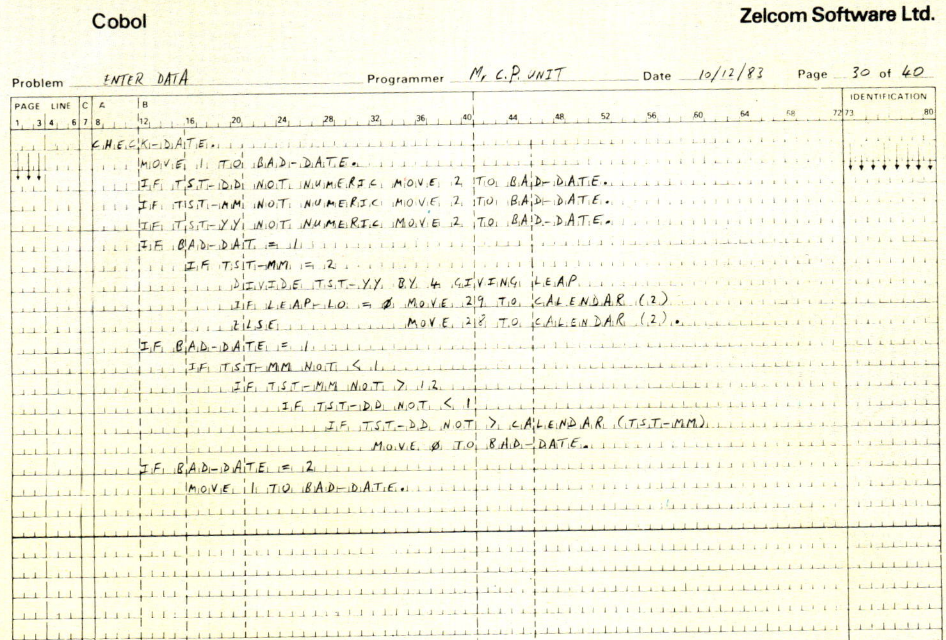

Cobol

Zelcom Software Ltd.

Problem ENTER DATA Programmer M, C.P. UNIT Date 10/12/83 Page 30 of 40

```
CHECK-DATE.
    MOVE 1 TO BAD-DATE.
    IF TST-DD NOT NUMERIC MOVE 2 TO BAD-DATE.
    IF TST-MM NOT NUMERIC MOVE 2 TO BAD-DATE.
    IF TST-YY NOT NUMERIC MOVE 2 TO BAD-DATE.
    IF BAD-DAT = 1
        IF TST-MM = 2
            DIVIDE TST-YY BY 4 GIVING LEAP
            IF LEAP-LO = Ø MOVE 29 TO CALENDAR (2)
            ELSE           MOVE 28 TO CALENDAR (2).
    IF BAD-DATE = 1
        IF TST-MM NOT < 1
            IF TST-MM NOT > 12
                IF TST-DD NOT < 1
                    IF TST-DD NOT > CALENDAR (TST-MM)
                        MOVE Ø TO BAD-DATE.
    IF BAD-DATE = 2
        MOVE 1 TO BAD-DATE.
```

PROGRAMMING

The computer will faithfully carry out our program instruction by instruction. The computer has no commonsense so it is up to the person writing the program to make sure that they have written down exactly what they want to happen and have allowed for every possibility.

The first stage in writing a program is to make sure that you understand exactly what you want the computer to do. This will involve writing down a detailed description in English. For example you cannot just tell a computer to do your maths homework. You will firstly have to understand exactly what needs to be done because you will have to tell the computer how to do it.

The next stage is to break down the task that the computer is to carry out into small steps. These steps are shown in a flowchart. A flowchart is a diagram that shows the sequence of actions in the correct order. Arrows indicate the order in which the actions take place.

Now you have to translate each step in the flowchart into the language you are using. This must be done very carefully, paying great attention to the rules of the language.

The written program can now be entered into the computer. This will usually be done through the keyboard. When the program is run for the first time there will probably be some mistakes in it. These are called bugs. They make the computer stop working or cause unwanted or the wrong things to happen. The bugs have to be corrected by finding which instructions are causing the problem and re-entering them correctly. The program can now be tested again and perhaps more bugs will show themselves, in which case you will have to go through the correction process again. In a large program it will take a lot of work before the program is thoroughly tested and all the bugs removed. This is known as de-bugging.

The main symbols used in a flow chart are:

A terminator box marks the beginning and end of a set of instructions.

An operation box contains an instruction to the computer.

A decision box contains a question. It usually has two paths leading from it, one for the answer "Yes" and one for the answer "No".

HERE IS A FLOWCHART FOR WASHING YOUR HANDS

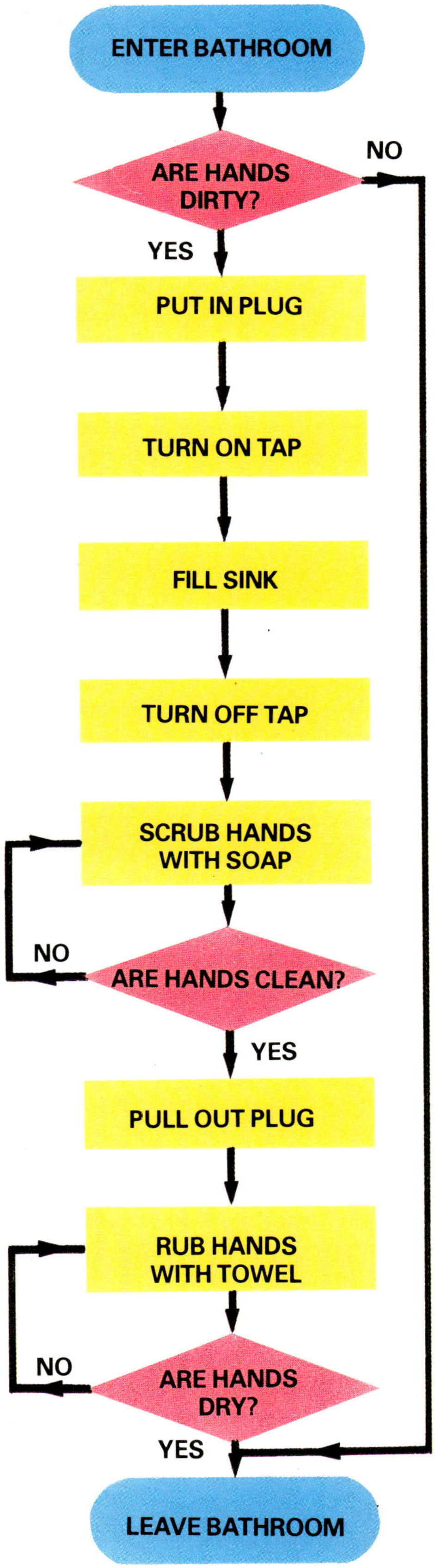

HERE IS A SMALL PROGRAM TO CALCULATE THE AREA OF A SQUARE

The area = side × side

FLOWCHART

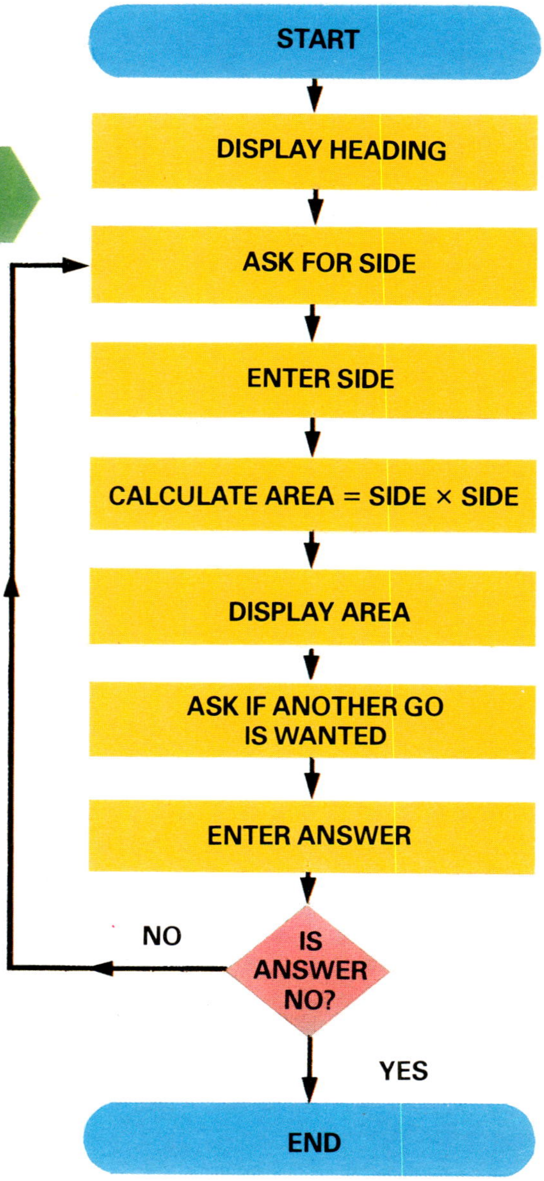

In this program each line is numbered 1Ø, 2Ø, 3Ø . . . We could have numbered each line 1, 2, 3, . . . but by allowing gaps of 10 we are able to squeeze extra instructions in later if we find it necessary. Zeros are written with a slash through them Ø so that there is no confusion with the letter O.

PRINT is an output instruction. It tells the computer to display something on the screen.
INPUT is an input instruction. It allows you to enter something through the keyboard.
This instruction calculates the area.
The * is the computer symbol for ×.
These two instructions are how the decision is programmed.
If the answer to "DO YOU WANT ANOTHER GO?" is "NO" you go to line 1ØØ to end.
Otherwise you go back to line 2Ø for another go.

PROGRAM (written in BASIC)

```
 1Ø PRINT "AREA OF A SQUARE"
 2Ø PRINT "WHAT IS LENGTH OF SIDE?"
 3Ø INPUT S
 4Ø LET A = S*S
 5Ø PRINT "THE AREA ="; A
 6Ø PRINT "DO YOU WANT ANOTHER
    GO?"
 7Ø INPUT A$
 8Ø IF A$ = "NO" THEN GOTO 1ØØ
 9Ø GOTO 2Ø
1ØØ END
```

HOW COMPUTERS WORK

The size of a computer's internal RAM memory is measured in bytes. A microcomputer can store between about 16,000 and 64,000 bytes. In computer jargon this would be written 16K to 64K. K stands for kilobyte which is 1024 bytes.

BINARY CODE

It might be difficult at first to see how a computer can do anything, because there are no moving parts inside the processor. However, there is electricity flowing around and this is what is used. We have mentioned at various places in this book that the processor can understand patterns of electronic pulses. Each pulse can be either at high voltage or low voltage, which is like on and off. We can think of the high voltage, or on, as 1 and low voltage, or off, as 0. So what we have is a code of 0s and 1s passing around inside the computer. This code is known as binary code.

Binary uses combinations of these two digits 0 and 1 to code all information. Everything from numbers and letters, even pictures, can be coded in this way.

Each 0 and 1 is called a 'bit', short for binary digit. We usually put bits into groups of eight and we call this group a 'byte'. The eight bits of a byte can make 256 different combinations of 0s and 1s, which is more than enough to represent each key on the keyboard.

Each byte contains the code for a particular character. A character can be:

a number from 0 to 9
a letter A B C D . . . or a b c d . . .
a symbol *, +. etc.

Some examples of the code are:

CHARACTER	BYTE 8 bits
A	01000001
B	01000010
C	01000011
D	01000100
E	01000101
F	01000110
0	00000000
1	00000001
2	00000010
3	00000011
4	00000100
5	00000101
*	00101010
	00101100

The computer can move bytes around its circuits and store them in the memory. The arithmetic and logic unit in the CPU can add them and compare them. To find out how this is done we will have to know some more about the binary code.

You can think of binary code as 'on' and 'off' light bulbs.

COUNTING IN BINARY

The decimal code, based on ten digits, is the one we generally use at school. When we count in decimal, we count from 0 up to 9 and then we "carry one" into the tens column: 0, 1, 2, 3, 4, 5, 6, 7, 8, 9, 10. When we count in binary which uses base two, we can only go as far as 1! We start off 0 . . . 1 and then we have to 'carry one' into the next column, the two's column, and put 0 in the units column. So after 1 we have 10. Counting up from 0 we get: 0, 1, 10, 11, 100, 101, 110, 111, 1000, 1001, etc.

Look at the table below.

Look at the table opposite.

Can you see a pattern building up?

DECIMAL BASE TEN	BINARY BASE TWO
0	0
1	1
2	10
3	11
4	100
5	101
6	110
7	111
8	1000
9	1001
10	1010

ADDITION IN BINARY

Don't be afraid, it's not as awful as it looks. The rules are 0 plus 0 is 0, 1 plus 0 is 1 and 1 plus 1 is 0 with 1 to carry.

Here are some examples of binary arithmetic:

$$\begin{array}{r} 1 \\ +\ 10 \\ 11 \end{array} \qquad \begin{array}{r} 11 \\ +\ 11 \\ 110 \end{array} \qquad \begin{array}{r} 101 \\ +\ 110 \\ 1011 \end{array} \qquad \begin{array}{r} 1010 \\ +\ 111 \\ 10001 \end{array}$$

To multiply the computer uses repeated addition. Subtraction is treated as the addition of negative numbers. Division is repeated subtraction. So all arithmetic can be done using only addition.

USING BINARY TO MAKE DECISIONS

The arithmetic and logic unit is built up of decision making blocks called logic gates. Basically a decision can be one of three types: AND, OR and NOT.

You can think of an AND decision in the situation where if you were going out AND it was cold you would put your coat on. You need to say "Yes" to "Are you going out?" AND "Yes" to "Is it cold?" before you say "Yes" to putting your coat on. An OR decision is of the type that when you go out, if it is raining OR looks like rain, you take your umbrella. A NOT decision arises if you decide NOT to go out if it is raining. A "Yes" answer to "Is it raining?" means a "No" answer to "Are you going out?"

Inside the ALU, electrical components within the chip are combined to form logic gates. There are three sorts of gate: AND-gate, OR-gate and NOT-gate. These make decisions similar to those discussed above, except that instead of yes/no answers it uses binary 1 and 0. Binary code in the form of electrical pulses is passed through the gates. Each AND-gate and OR-gate has two inputs through which it receives a signal. A NOT-gate has one input. Each gate sends out one signal through its output. The signal passing out of a gate depends on the code it has received and the sort of gate it is.

AND-GATE

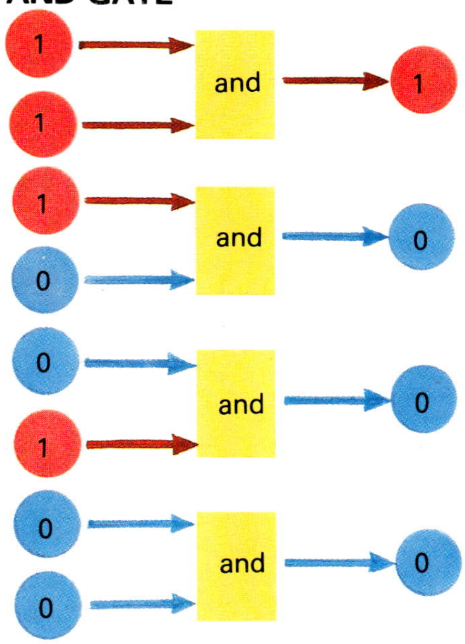

The AND-gate has two inputs. It sends out a binary 1 only if it receives a binary 1 on both its inputs.

OR-GATE

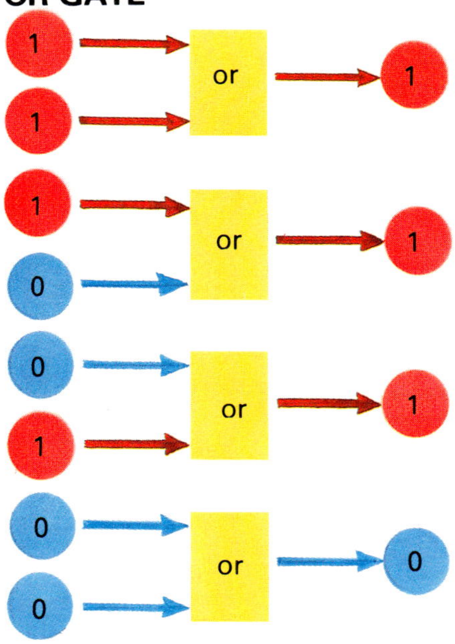

The OR-gate has two inputs. It sends out a binary 1 if it receives a binary 1 at either or both of its inputs.

is raining
ɔ I am **NOT** going out

NOT-GATE

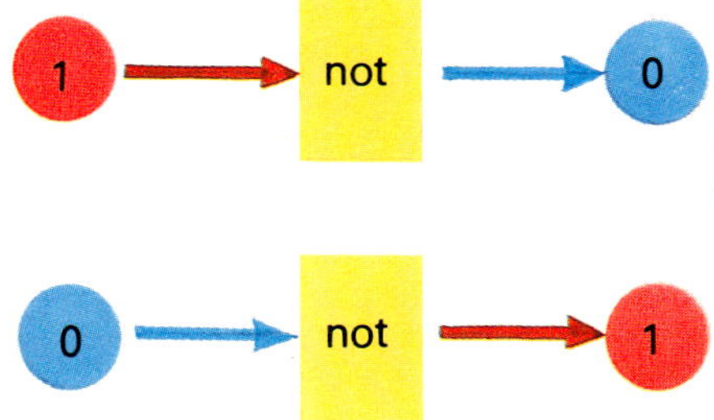

The NOT-gate has one input. It sends out the opposite of what it receives. If it receives 0 it sends out 1. If it receives 1 it sends out 0.

HOW LOGIC GATES ARE USED

Logic gates are combined together into logic circuits. Some circuits can do binary arithmetic. For example this diagram shows the gates needed to add two binary digits. It is shown adding 1 to 1 but will work whatever its inputs are. It is known as a half adder.

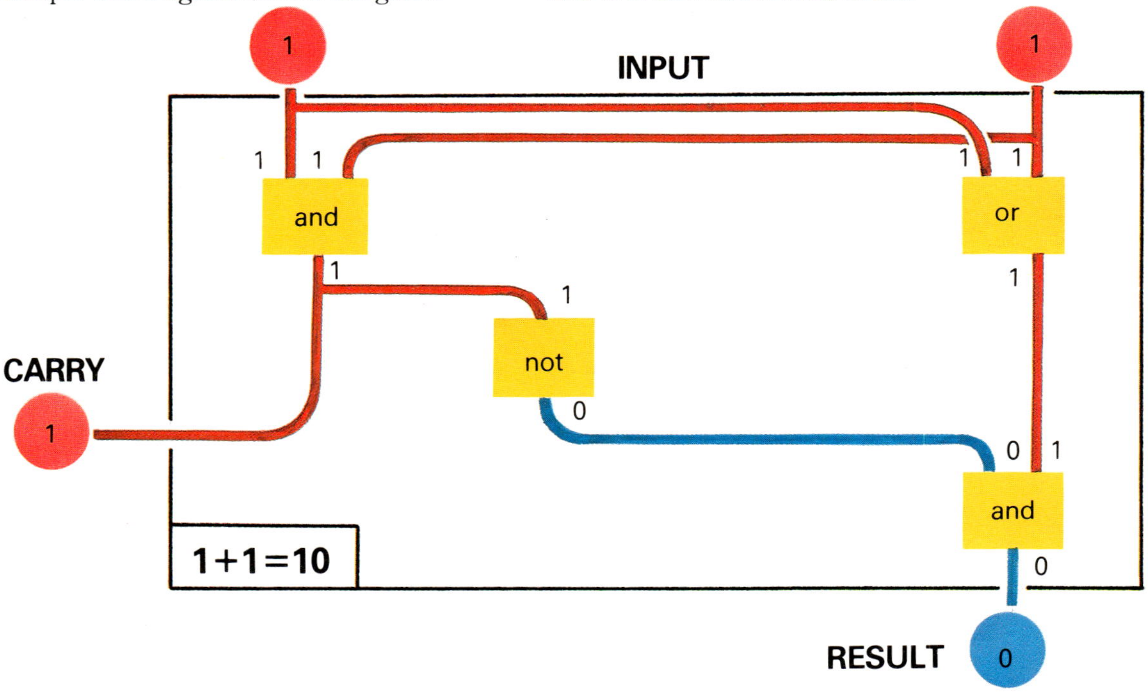

Gates can also be combined to allow the arithmetic unit to do logical operations. For example, this diagram shows how gates can be combined to compare two binary digits. The result is 1 if the two digits are different or 0 if they are the same. It is shown comparing 1 to 0.

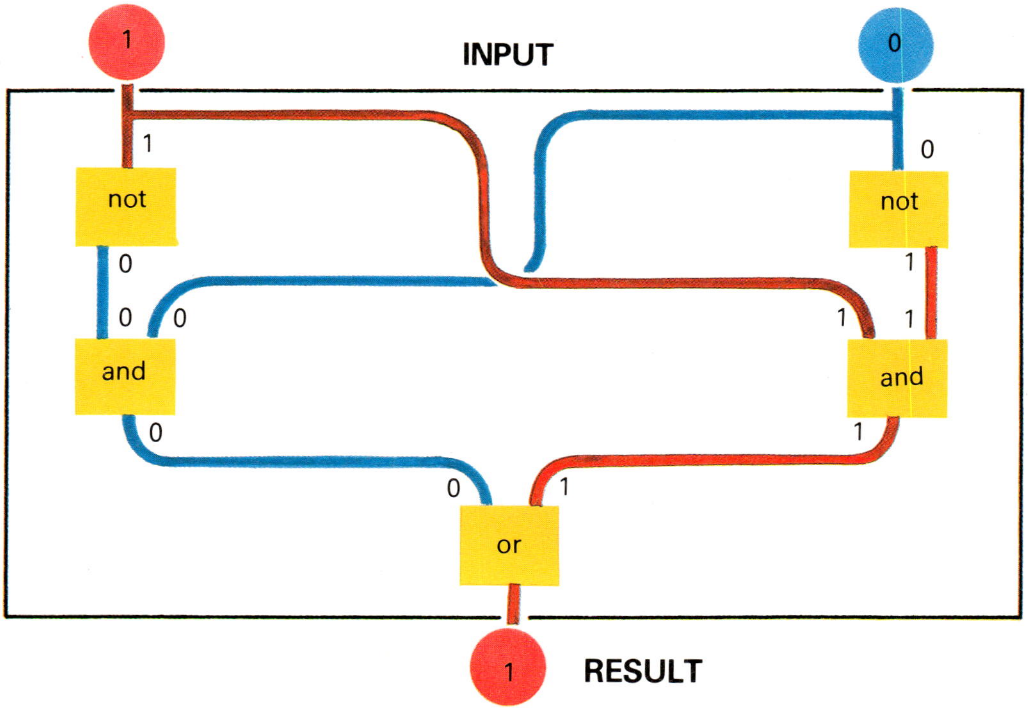

You should now have some idea how the ALU goes about its task, but remember the examples you have seen here are simple ones and the circuits in a real ALU are extremely complicated. The larger the computer the more complicated they are.

COMPUTERS EVERYWHERE

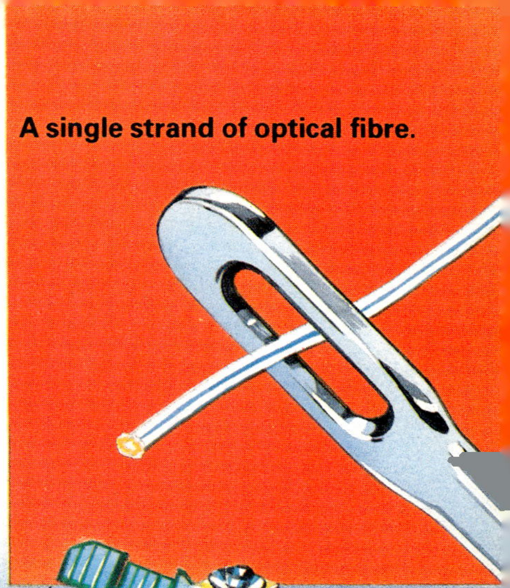

A single strand of optical fibre.

The first working computers were built in the 1940s. Since then progress has been rapid. Today, computers are found everywhere. They are not only much smaller but also cheaper, more powerful, more reliable and easier to use than computers of yesterday. The development of the microcomputer has meant that small businesses and even families are finding that they can well afford to buy their own computer.

In commerce, industry, air travel, medicine and scientific and technological research we have come to depend on computers. They are used increasingly in offices, in schools and in the home.

Using the telephone and a modem you can speak to the computer in your office from an hotel room anywhere in the world.

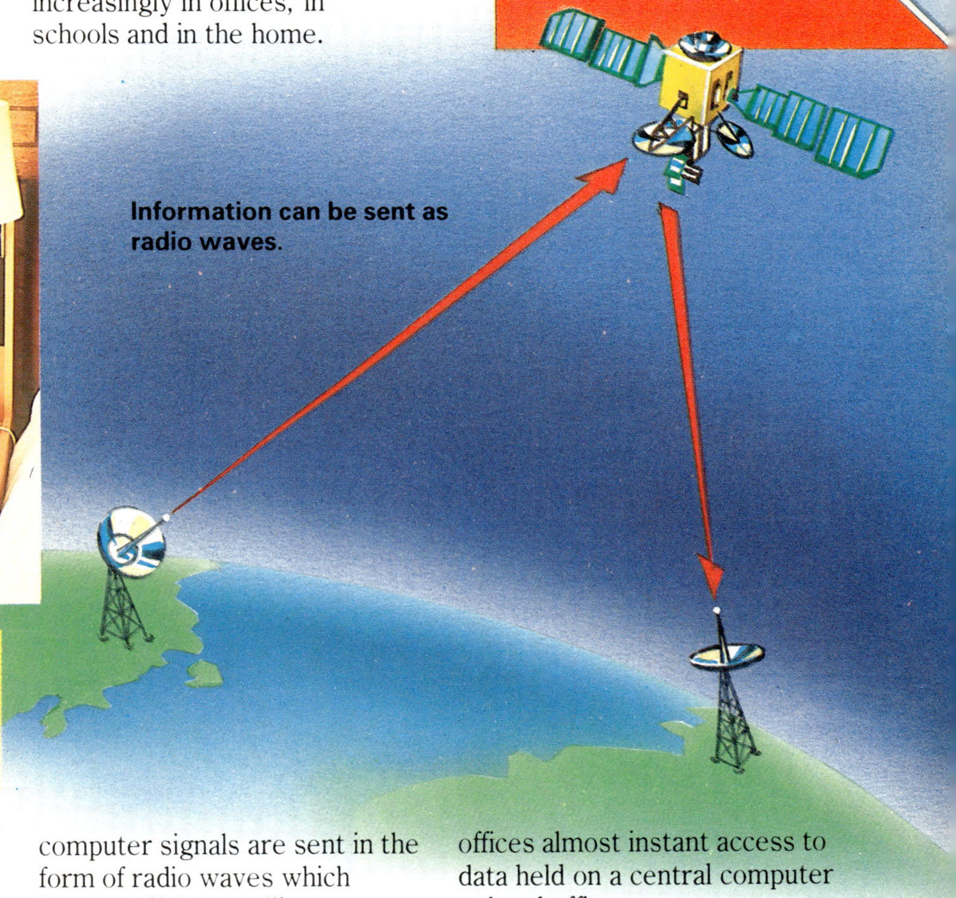

Information can be sent as radio waves.

COMPUTER NETWORKS

When computers are linked together to talk or communicate with each other it is called a network. A computer network can operate within a single building or across the world.

A network can be linked by telephone using a modem. This device can change electronic signals from the computer into the kinds of signals that telephone lines can carry.

Over long distances networks can be linked by satellite, in which case computer signals are sent in the form of radio waves which bounce off the satellite.

The development of fibre optic cable is a major advance in communication networks. An optical fibre is a thread of very pure glass, so fine that it could fit through the eye of a needle. Electronic signals from the computer are translated into laser light signals and as such can be sent through the optical fibre.

Large national companies use computer network systems. The network allows computers, known as terminals, in branch offices almost instant access to data held on a central computer at head office.

The network can be used to provide an electronic mail service. Business letters can be typed out on the keyboard and sent to another computer where the letter is left on the screen.

Through a network system a large computer can be used by many different companies at the same time. In this way companies can share the cost of running a large mainframe computer.

The British Airways Passenger services system is one of the largest computer networks in the world, consisting of over 50 computers linked to 3,500 VDUs and 1,000 teleprinters in 650 cities! Agents within the network can find out instantly what seats are available on any aeroplane anywhere in the world.

Through a network computers can be linked up to information centres which we call databanks. British Telecom's Prestel is a large public computer which acts like a databank, storing information on a vast range of subjects. Prestel signals travel along the ordinary telephone line and into a special TV set which can decode them. A keypad allows you to call up 'pages' of information and it also allows you to talk back to the TV set, for instance by keying in your credit card number you can shop at home.

Within a network terminals are linked to a mainframe.

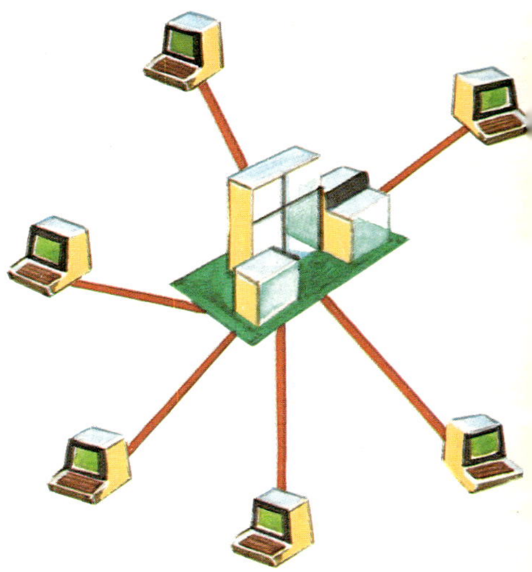

Computers at mission control.

COMPUTERS IN SPACE TRAVEL

Space exploration would be totally unthinkable without computers. They calculate, plan and control every minute detail at each stage in a space flight.

On board they control take-off, flight course, speed, fuel supply, engine systems, life-support systems, communications with earth, emergency back-up and soft landings.

At mission control larger computers constantly monitor the spacecraft's activities and process the information which is sent back to them.

COMPUTERS IN AIR TRAVEL

Airlines use computer technology to control almost every aspect of their operations.

Travel agents use a computer network system to check seats on aeroplanes, availability on package holidays, rooms in hotels and to make bookings. Computers even work out fares and issue tickets.

At the airport the person behind the check-in desk uses a computer to register the arrival of the passenger, to reserve a seat on the aeroplane and to document the luggage. Computers draw up airline timetables, direct flights to and from the airport, control cargo and fuel supply, monitor engine and safety systems, work out airmail and freight accounts, organise flight planning, supply in-flight data and even fly the aircraft. Computers are also assisting in the training of pilots.

The cockpit with its complicated instrument panel is simulated (drawn realistically) on the screen. The trainee simply touches the display screen to activate the instruments.

COMPUTERS PREDICTING THE WEATHER

In order to forecast the weather in the UK for just a few days ahead it is necessary to observe and predict developments over most of the world. To do this some of the world's most powerful computers are used.

The London Weather Centre receives $1\frac{1}{2}$ million observations each day from points both on land and sea covering a large area of the earth's surface. In addition, there are aircraft reports and satellite data that need to be analysed. Using this enormous amount of information mathematical calculations are carried out by computer to produce forecasts of wind, rainfall, temperature, pressure and humidity at fifteen different levels above the ground and at one third of a million points around the world. From this our daily weather forecast is produced.

But weather forecasts on television and radio are only a very small part of the activities of the Meteorological Office. The London Weather Centre provides a vital service for aviation, shipping, agriculture and construction industries. Forecasters work with computers around the clock to provide forecasts of wind, waves and weather for the oil and gas platforms in the North Sea.

Besides predicting day to day changes of weather, computers are being used to model or simulate longer term changes of climate. Given information about world weather patterns the computer can work out a model in the form of a description in words, charts or graphs, of what would happen if, for instance, the polar ice was melted.

The weather forecast is entered into the Prestel databank to be received on television sets.

Weather chart being plotted

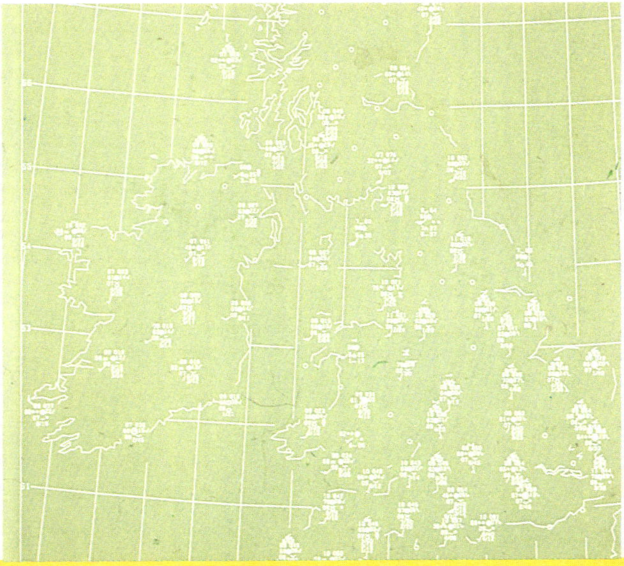

Computer plotted surface chart

An office micro system

COMPUTERS IN OFFICES

Every working day in thousands of offices secretaries are busily typing letters, documents and reports upon millions of pieces of paper. In the future, word processors could take over the whole operation.

Instead of using a typewriter that puts your words on paper, you could type those words into a computer which displays them on a screen and allows you to make any number of corrections before you write anything on paper. Using a pointer on the screen, you can move words around, replace words and correct spelling errors. When you're happy with the text the computer can store the final draft. A printer linked to the computer can produce perfect copies as and when you require them.

Word processors can also help with filing. As information is entered into the computer it can automatically work out an index in its memory, so that a particular piece of information can be found almost immediately and then displayed or printed out as required.

The next step, of course, would be to send this information electronically. Computer mail systems are faster than paper mailings and cost less.

But it is in the accounts office that computers have moved furthest. All accounts that were once held in a filing cabinet are now handled by computers. They are being used to keep records of stock, money spent and money received and to forecast future sales. Bills and receipts are produced by computers and they are used to keep records of employees and to produce payslips.

COMPUTERS IN SHOPS

The bar-coding system is being used by some supermarkets with many goods now bar-coded. At the checkout, instead of the assistant finding the price tag and keying the amount into the till, the process is done automatically as the bar-code is read by passing the goods over a special reader which contains a laser beam. The reader is linked to a computer and the number identifies the item and its price.

For the customer this means faster service and a receipt which shows exactly what we have spent our money on. For the assistants it means that they are relieved of the tiresome task of stamping prices on hundreds of items. The checkout automatically records sales so the manager can see how each product is selling. Transmit this information to the warehouse and you can trigger a re-order as soon as stocks fall.

Bar codes are read by a special reader

An operator using a Cheque Reader Sorter

COMPUTERS IN BANKING

Every working day banks handle and process an enormous quantity of information, in the form of cheques, salaries, bills, deposits, savings, overdrafts, loans . . . all of which involves the transfer of millions of pieces of paper between banks and customers' accounts. This volume of information would be totally unmanageable without the help of computers.

Right from the start banking has made full use of computers. Activities such as book-keeping, accounting, reading and sorting of cheques have for a long time relied upon automation.

In the early 1960s with the development of magnetic ink character recognition (MCR) it was possible to sort out cheques rapidly and automatically using a special reader.

Today computer screens and terminals are seen everywhere. Automatic cash tills provide a service 24 hours a day, 7 days a week. These computers allow you to draw cash, check the balance in your account and order a cheque book.

For the transfer of money from one country to another nearly 1,000 banks in 40 countries are linked in a computer based network. Using satellite and cable transmission, messages can be sent from bank to bank across the world at high speed.

Computer technology seems to be taking us steadily towards a society where we don't need money in our pockets, the so-called 'cashless' society. Some banks have already introduced point of sale terminals in shops (POS). The idea is that the customer, on paying for goods in a shop, would simply insert a plastic card into an electronic reader at the checkout and key in their personal identification number; then the shop's computer, which is linked to the reader, would automatically debit the customer's account and credit the shop's account.

Banking from home is another possibility in the near future. Banks already provide information on Prestel, if this system was linked directly to the bank's computers then, using a keypad and a television set that received Prestel, we could call up statements of our accounts and make simple payments.

Customers using the automatic cash till. It's open even when the bank isn't!

Cashiers in banks and building societies sometimes have their own terminals linked directly to the main computer at head office.

ROBOTICS

CP30

Robot welders on an automatic car production line.

Robots such as CP30, from the film *Star Wars,* modelled on the human form, that can move freely, can see, can talk, can understand conversation, can have their own opinions and personalities only exist in the world of science fiction. In reality given present technology the robot is a mechanical device, often just a single arm, that is specialised in a particular task.

Computer-controlled robots are playing an important part in modern industry, particularly in car manufacture where the entire production line can be automated. They are replacing human workers in jobs that are heavy and tedious or that are carried out in dangerous and unpleasant surroundings.

Robots are good workers, they can repeat routine tasks time after time, never tire and never become bored or careless. They are cheaper to employ and never go on strike.

But on the other hand even the simplest task for us is difficult for a robot and the necessary instructions are immensely long and complex. In some applications, such as paint spraying, the computer can be 'taught' how to do a job in the following way. Firstly a human worker goes through the process using the robotic arm and the computer 'remembers' all the movements. It can then repeat the same cycle of actions endlessly.

The robot is not as adaptable as the human worker it has replaced, so that when you want to alter its function you often have to completely redesign the robot. Also, a robot isn't capable of making decisions and when something happens that is unexpected it doesn't know how to deal with it.

Nevertheless the range of operations which robots can handle is increasing and it is likely that in the future they will become more adaptable.

Some people fear that robots will lead to increased unemployment and they oppose their use in all areas, but others argue that by increasing industrial production robots will give workers more leisure time. It remains to be seen.

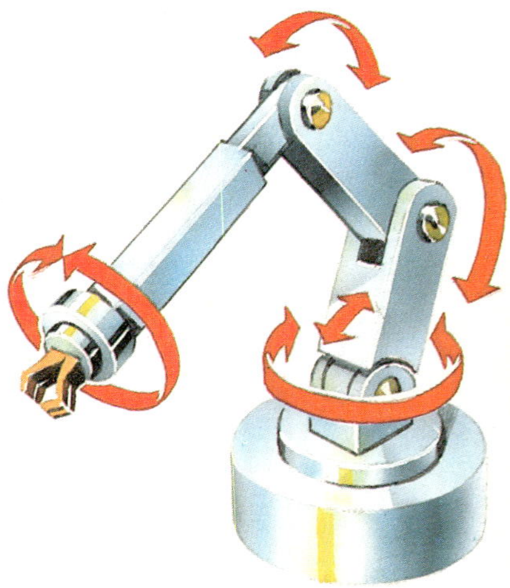

A robot can usually rotate from five "joints" – the waist, shoulder, elbow, wrist and hand.

COMPUTER GRAPHICS

When we talk about computer 'graphics' we are referring to the ability of the computer to draw or build up pictures on the screen. The demand for good graphics is increasing and this area is at present the fastest developing.

Computer graphics techniques are being applied to the making of cartoons in the film industry. The illusion of 'moving pictures' is created by drawing a series of action sequences which, when run at speed, appear to move. This is known as animation. In the past an artist would have spent hundreds of hours working out hundreds of separate drawings for just one piece of action. Today such tiresome work can be done quite easily and much more quickly with a computer.

Taking together high resolution, animation, and 3-D capabilities spectacular effects can be produced.

The exciting and powerful visual effects used in Walt Disney's *Tron* were computer drawn.

Computer graphics are being applied in a variety of different areas from educational and games software to simulations, computer aided design and photographic analysis.

COMPUTER AIDED DESIGN

CAD helping design shoes.

Aerospace, motor manufacture and electronic industries are using Computer Aided Design (CAD) systems to develop new products.

The computer can draw up a realistic model of the new design on the screen and it can make sure that each part of the design is strong enough for the job it has to do, making it no longer necessary to build an expensive test model. The computer can give a breakdown of all the materials needed for production and can even design the machine tools that will make the parts. Speeding up the design stage means that new products are developed more quickly and cheaply than ever before and this enables industries to keep up with present demands and fashions.

Architects are using CAD systems to help design costly new buildings. CAD can be of great assistance here in that it allows you to see what the building will look like before it is actually built. By using a sequence of pictures on the screen that are adjusted to the eye level of the viewer, you can 'walk through' the building and be shown rooms from every possible angle as if you were really there. CAD has been used in the building of hospitals, office blocks and North Sea oil rigs.

COMPUTERS IN MEDICINE

Within medicine computers are being used everywhere. At the simplest level, storing a patient's medical records in the computer's memory leads to their easier access and quicker consultation, thus saving everyone a great deal of time.

Computers are very good at 'nursing' people because they can keep a constant watch over patients. They can give accurate information concerning a patient's condition by monitoring bodily functions such as heart beat and breathing. By comparing this with information which is taken from the healthy they can identify possible problems and help doctors make the right decisions about a patient's treatment.

Computers control all kinds of medical equipment. There are body scanners that can take photographs of the organs inside the body and computer based systems that help look after premature babies.

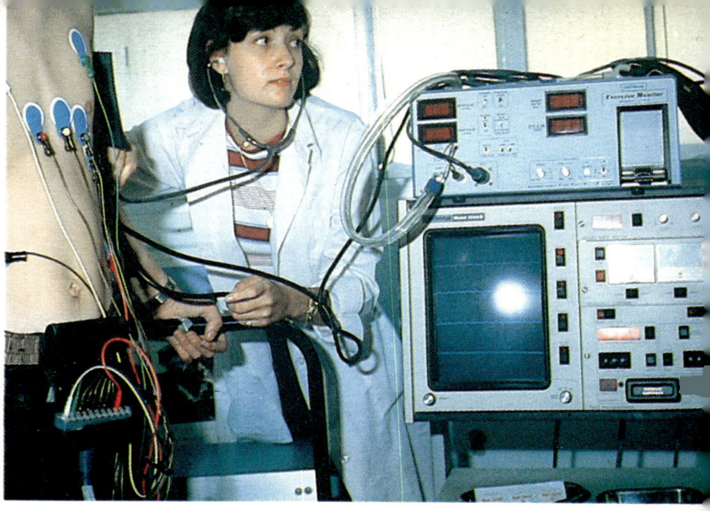

Patient wired up to computer monitoring equipment.

Doctors are now using computers to help in the diagnosis of illness. To do this the doctor collects information from the patient and details of symptoms and types this into the computer. Comparing this data with information and symptoms stored in its memory of real medical case histories the computer can give a diagnosis and also suggest possible methods of treatment.

In surgery, computers have made possible techniques that were inconceivable before and that have helped save many lives. For instance there are pacemakers that can actually imitate and replace the body's natural heart functions.

An important application of computer technology is with the disabled. It can mean that via the computer keyboard they are really in control and able to communicate with the outside world. This in turn can give insight on their condition to doctors.

At a more routine level, in the chemist shop computers are keeping stock of drugs and printing labels.

Computers are an invaluable help in medical research.

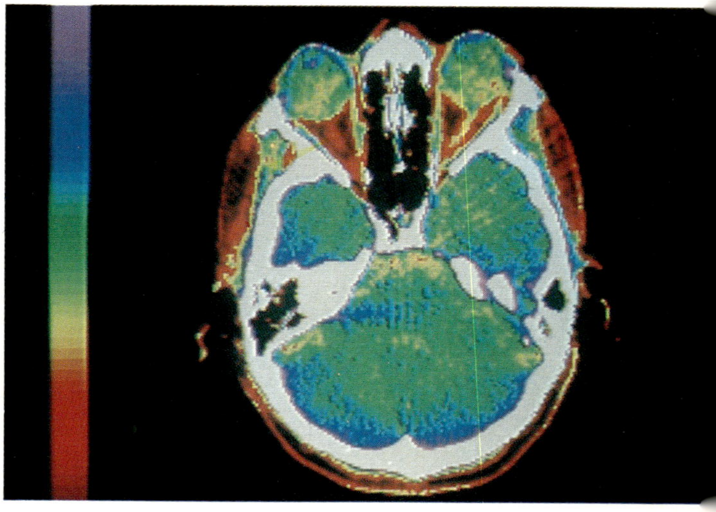

A computer-produced x-ray photograph of a section through the human skull.

The force control room at headquarters.

COMPUTERS AND THE POLICE

The Police National Computer now provides all police forces in England, Scotland and Wales with immediate access, day and night, to an increasing amount of up-to-date information about crime and criminals.

Information held on the computer is in the form of separate indexes, each dealing with a particular subject. The information is designed to help police officers decide on the correct course of action. There is an index of all vehicle owners, a file which lists stolen or suspect vehicles, an index to criminal names, a wanted and missing persons file, a disqualified drivers file and a finger print file.

At the local level too computer systems are being used. Increasingly, all 999 calls will be received at Local Headquarters where officers input the information directly into a computer, which automatically numbers and times the calls. The computer will then search its Street Index File and identify the area containing the incident. It will look through its Resource Availability File and choose which resource – foot patrol, cars, accident units to send. Details of resources sent, action taken and later the result will be stored.

The advantages of this system are many. Sending out the right sort of help at the right time is important. It means that incidents can be handled quickly and effectively, reducing risk and providing a better service to the public.

But of greatest importance is the need to maintain the privacy and security of the police files. There is a fear that files held on computer could be accessed by the wrong people. For this reason the possibility of extending the use of computers within the local police force is being very cautiously approached.

Computers provide a vast amount of information just a call away.

COMPUTERS IN SCHOOLS

Almost all schools now have at least one microcomputer which is being used to help children learn and to help teachers teach. Computers are being used both to support and extend the range of subjects taught in schools. Learning how to control a computer – 'computer literacy' – is now as vital as learning how to read and write.

A history lesson.

The Buggy.

Computers can make learning fun; unlike teachers they have infinite patience and always give immediate replies. They can be programmed to help with almost any subject.

But it is not only the children who benefit. A computer is a powerful teaching aid, it is like having another teacher in the classroom. Computer graphics can often clarify in a few seconds what might take the teacher half a lesson to explain in another way.

Computers are used in schools to give practice in basic skills; there are graded spelling, English and maths programs. In some schools word processing programs are being used to help children with their writing.

There are educational games programs that are designed to help children develop their thinking and to make learning more fun. For example, adventure programs use simulations and models to create a rich, imaginary world, one difficult to provide in any other way, in which the child is in control, making all decisions themselves and later learning the consequence of those decisions!

Some children are being taught programming languages such as LOGO and BASIC. There are programmable toys that can help pupils learn how to control computers and use simple programming languages. The BBC Buggy is one example. The Buggy, when linked to a micro, is a kind of robot that can do a number of difficult tasks. It can be driven simply by using the keys on the keyboard or you can plan a route for the Buggy to follow.

Programming a toy.

Using the word processor.

COMPUTERS IN THE HOME

The development of the microcomputer has meant that anyone can learn to use a computer, they need not be a scientist or mathematician, and a child who can recognise letters and numbers will quickly learn how to operate a computer. Today, individuals are now finding that they can easily afford to buy their own home computer. Indeed, many parents are buying 'micros' as presents for their children; they are seen as an investment in their child's future. Computers are now becoming a familiar sight in our homes, so what are we all doing with them?

Many of us are playing games. Computers are marvellously entertaining and there is a wide and growing range of software available to help us do almost anything. You can defend the Earth from attacking aliens, dodge planetoids, seek lost treasure, explore magical worlds of goblins and dragons or face a dangerous mission as the nation's top secret agent, not to mention playing traditional games like chess and draughts.

But as well as being entertaining a computer can educate us: you can test your general knowledge, improve your maths and spelling and even learn to write your own programs. A computer is also valuable for home management: by keeping track of family spending or storing addresses or recipes. In the future it is possible that many of us will be able to work from home, bank from home, shop by computer catalogue, and so on.

Even if you don't have a microcomputer yet, it is very likely that you have an electronic toy or calculator that contains a microprocessor chip. Microprocessors now control all kinds of equipment found in the home, because not only are they extremely reliable but they also make equipment easier to use. Washing machines use microprocessors to control their washing cycles and water temperatures, sewing machines to remember hundreds of stitching patterns. Central heating systems now use chips to control when they come on and go off. Using microprocessors, cameras can adjust themselves automatically to take better pictures. Even digital watches, those with alarms and calculators, contain microprocessors.

HERE TO STAY

There is no doubt that computer technology will continue to develop, producing smaller and more powerful computers which will find an ever increasing number of applications in society.

Computers will certainly continue to replace thousands of workers. Some people would argue that for many this is for the better, because it frees them from jobs that were either repetitive or dangerous, and for all it could mean the opportunity to be more creative in another field. Others protest that increased automation will merely lead to increased unemployment.

On the other hand, computer technology will create new job opportunities in the future in work that is directly related to computers and their application. If people were more adaptable and prepared to accept change then with re-training they could take up these opportunities.

One worry is that an increasing amount of information about each of us will be held in huge databanks; some argue that this is an invasion of our privacy and fear that this information could be obtained by the wrong people for the wrong purposes. For this reason there will be a need for much stricter security in the future.

Looking on the bright side, computers will bring increased production which could mean that we spend less time at work and have more leisure time for sports and hobbies.

Entertainment is an area where new developments are on the horizon. Games are becoming more sophisticated and soon we may even be able to star in our favourite film.

In many areas such as medicine, as we have seen, computer technology is giving us an opportunity to improve the quality of our lives.

The question is where will it end? Whatever the outcome, computer technology will have a profound effect on the way we work, live and think. We will be forced to reconsider our traditional values and attitudes in so many ways.

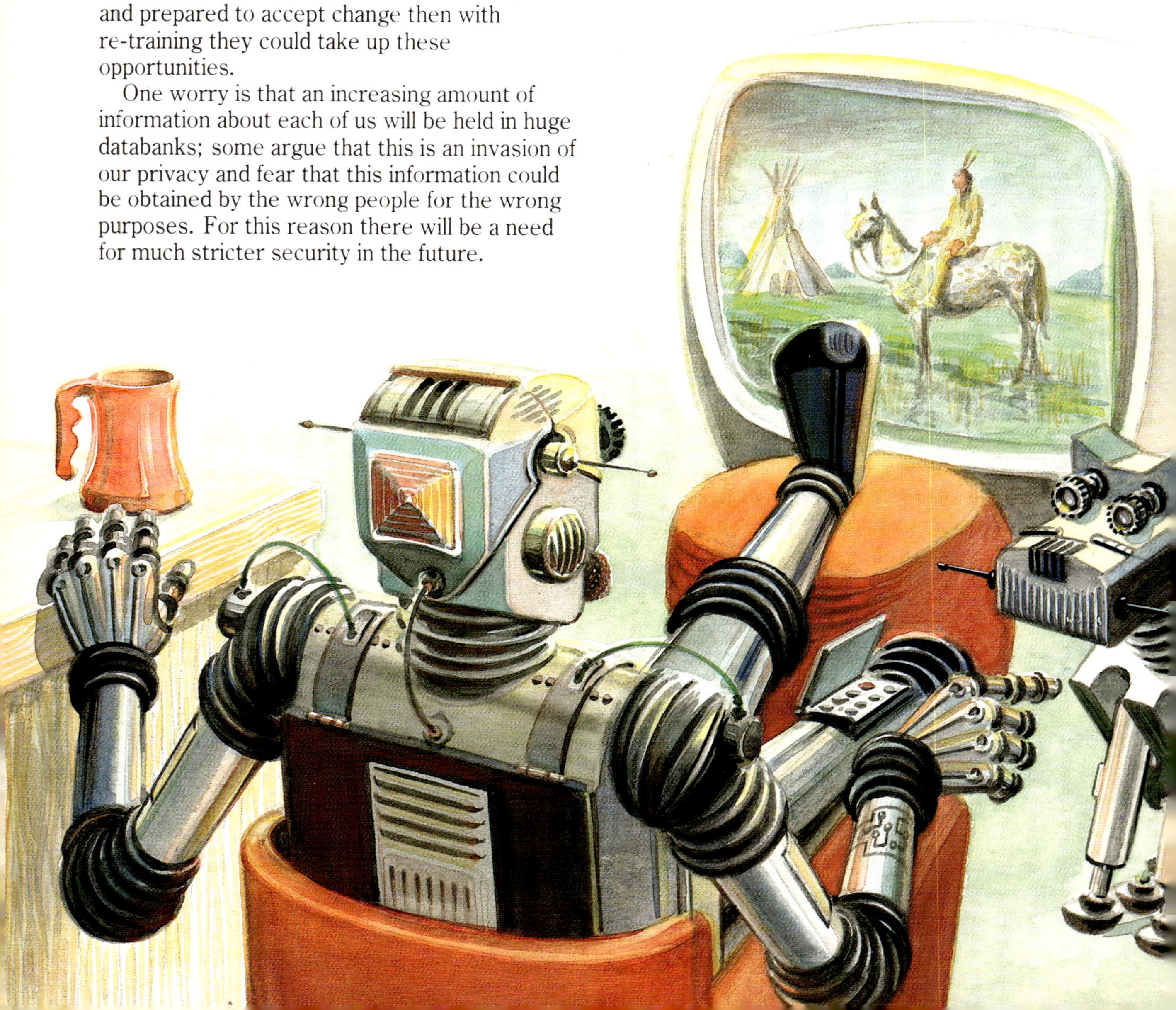

COMPUTER DICTIONARY

Address The number given to each part of the internal *memory* to allow its contents to be found.

Arithmetic and Logic Unit (ALU) The part of the *central processing unit* where arithmetic and comparisons are performed.

Bar Code A patch of black and white stripes on the packaging of goods which identifies the product to a laser scanner in a computerized check-out in a supermarket or shop.

BASIC A *programming language* which is popular for microcomputers.

Binary A system of counting that only uses the numbers 0 and 1. Binary is represented inside the computer by pulses of electricity that are off (0) or on (1).

Bit A *binary* digit, 0 or 1.

Bug A mistake in a computer *program.*

Bus An electrical pathway along which *data* is moved around inside the computer.

Byte A group of eight *bits* which form the computer code for a *character.*

Central processing unit (CPU) The part of the computer where information is processed and which links and controls the other parts.

Character A letter, number or symbol.

Chip A small piece of silicon containing electronic circuits.

Control unit The part of the *central processing unit* that directs its operation.

Data Information which is used or produced by a computer.

Database or Databank A large organised collection of information available for use by a computer.

Disk A circular sheet of material with a magnetic surface which is used to store information as part of a computer's external *memory.* It has to be put in a disk drive to be used by the computer.

Flowchart When writing a *program* it is helpful to draw a diagram showing the steps involved. This is known as a flowchart.

Graphics Pictures or diagrams produced by a computer.

Hardware A piece of computer equipment that you can touch.

Input Anything put into the computer. An input unit such as a keyboard is used to put the information in.

Interface A device which converts electronic code to allow two pieces of a computer system to connect together.

Kilobyte (K) One kilobyte or 1K is 1024 bytes.

Machine code The code of on/off electric pulses which the computer works in.

Mainframe A large, powerful computer.

Memory Parts of the computer where information can be stored. Internal memory units such as *ROM* and *RAM* units store *data* and instructions the computer needs for its current *program.* External memory such as *disks* provide long term storage.

Microcomputer (Micro) A small computer such as that found in the home or in schools.

Microprocessor A *central processor unit* built within a single *chip.*

Minicomputer A computer between a *microcomputer* and a *mainframe* in size and power.

Modem A device which converts the computer's electronic code into a form which can pass down telephone wires.

Network A system in which computers are linked and are able to communicate with each other.

Output Any result given by the computer. The result will be presented through an output unit such as the screen.

Program language A set of instructions for a computer written in a *programming language.*

Programming Language A special language such as *BASIC* in which computer instructions are written and which can be translated into *machine code.*

Random Access Memory (RAM) Part of the internal *memory* where information is stored temporarily.

Read Only Memory (ROM) Part of the internal *memory* which stores information permanently.

Software *Programs* and *data* for the computer.

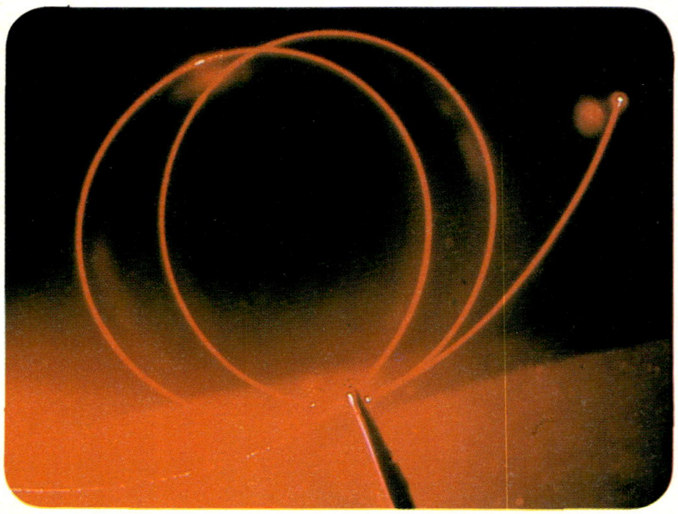

UNITED REV
JUSTIN SLEE

INTRODUCTION	04
LEEDS UNITED DESERVED A HERO	16
FOREVER & EVER, WE'LL FOLLOW OUR TEAM	40
HISTORY REPEATING MYSELF	58
MANAGING TO SUCCEED	82
OUR THING	102
MARCELO BIELSA BEATS AN UNSHAKABLE SENSE OF DOOM	118
VIEW FROM THE HILL	134
SOCK TAGS, SKOL & JIMMY ARMFIELD'S PIPE	152
HOW MUCH DO YOU THINK YOU'VE SPENT SUPPORTING LEEDS?	170
ACKNOWLEDGEMENTS	179

United Revolución
Justin Slee

unitedrevolucion.co.uk
justinslee.co.uk

ISBN: 978 1 5272 8051 9
First Edition

Printed in the UK by Jump North on FSC® certified paper

Designed by saul studio
saulstudio.co.uk

Typefaces
Komu A
URW Form
URW Form Expanded

Logistics evolved
Clipper
www.clippergroup.co.uk
Clipper
Clipper
Global
globalautocare.co

INTRODUCTION

As a very small child one of my earliest memories was having a blue tracksuit. Not a branded fashion statement by today's standards. Just a plain cotton tracksuit with the curly scripted LUFC logo on the front.

They say you always remember your first time. The finer details may be a little cloudy but there is always a moment that stays with you for life. Mine was on a cold winter evening sometime in the late 70s early 80s. I was quite old for my first game maybe, 10 or 11. I loved football, I played every day, every playtime and after school until I was shouted in. I lived with my mum, and back then dads took their sons to Elland Road. Football matches were supposed to be not for girls. All men together, it was a time of terrace hooligans, a working class sport with too much swearing and a feeling of violence in the air. These are not my thoughts; I was brought up in a happy home with a hard working mum with the help of my nana Jean. It was all things female and equal in our house, that was just the way it was back then. It was a different time and I just had to wait a little longer than most until Les, my mum's partner eventually took me.

Manchester United played under the floodlights, what a first time. The score 1–1 I think (I did mention details would be vague.) The goalscorers and the match statistics I have no idea. The moment engraved in my memory that night, was watching in mouth-opening awe, the Police in full riot gear, some on horseback chasing the Leeds fans up Beeston Hill. From that moment I was hooked. I was a Leeds fan for life. For the good and the bad and there has been plenty of bad.

For me being a Leeds supporter is unique. It's a lifetime of being very proud and sometimes embarrassed all at the same time. You are brought up with the 'Dirty Leeds' tag earned way back in the 60s and 70s, when lets be honest if you watch the Leeds Vs Chelsea 1970 FA Cup Final, Chelsea could have easily earned the same nick name. Everybody hates us, the Media, seemingly all of the opposition and their supporters and of course the Football Leagues corrupt. For me the conspiracy theories are all part of the Leeds United appeal. It cultivates the togetherness, 'We are Leeds!' the pump of the chest salute and the 'Marching on Together' terrace anthem that is sung worldwide. "You're a one City Club," we hear many times. "You should have great support". I would argue it is a lot easier if you are from a multi team city. You have a choice. Being a Leeds fan there is no choice, well except maybe Rugby League. It is an institution and once you are in, there is no getting out.

Over history we have had some amazing sides. Every football fan knows of Don Revie's team. It was the greatest in our story but Strachan and company were not bad either and more recently O'Leary's young team with Mark Viduka up front nearly delivered. We are supporters that take pride from those periods and dream for them to return.

We can endure the grim times too. Even in dark days we can find joy mixed with a dowdy, miserable togetherness. We amuse ourselves and share comedic moments about cult heroes in the likes of Carlton Palmer and Thomas Brolin. I have a friend Paul, (Brummie) a West Brom fan. He has lived in Leeds longer than he has lived in Smethwick. He loves to say "Leeds United are a club that shone brightly for a very short time." I like to respond, "Better to shine brightly now and again even if only for a little while, than never at all." Leeds United was the greatest club team in the land even if for only a short time. We love to argue, who is the bigger club? Deep down he knows really.

I have been fortunate that my career as a photographer has given me some great experiences with my team. One of my first assignments was covering the First Division Championship trophy being presented at Elland Road in 1992. It was not the firework spectacle like today's standard; it just involved our Captain walking out with the silverware before that Season's final game. I was subsequently with the team during the amazing open top bus parade through the city. I also once somehow slipped by Jack (a loveable ex fire officer the club employed as security) and persuaded manager Howard Wilkinson to allow me to photograph training so I could work on a feature about Tony Yeboah. I even managed to get Yeboah to agree to do an interview in the back of his car, days after those wonderful goals he smashed in against Liverpool and Wimbledon.

I also came close to burning down the West Stand once while photographing the Chief (Lucas Radebe) surrounded by candles for a Christmas card. All great experiences, the pinnacle of which was becoming the official magazine photographer for the club's *Leeds Leeds Leeds* magazine gaining weekly access to that great Champions League team. These were great times.

Nowadays, I am still a photographer but my daily work with the club ended around the same time Peter Ridsdale's fish tank left the stadium boardroom. Over the years your priorities change and now in my 50s the modern game and the reliance of finances in football has dampened the enthusiasm. I guess I had developed an acceptance and a feeling of football melancholy. The dark times had set in and it was going to take something godlike to spark and reignite my flame.

Sunday the 5th August 2018, my son Curtis offered me a ticket to go with him to Elland Road. (I think his friend had something better to do). It had been some time since I had been in person. It was a beautiful day and the first fixture of a new season. I did not expect much and knew nothing about the new head coach Marcelo Bielsa.
The previous season had been turbulent on and off the field and the club had finished 13th, a great distance away from the goal of promotion. I was just looking forward to a day out with my lad. Having a pint, some chips and curry sauce and maybe avoid a first game defeat. We arrived

to our seats via the bar and ten minutes before kick off. I stood and looked around the stadium. It always looks its best at that time of year. The pitch was immaculate and the ground was almost full. (Attendance 34,126 not bad for the Championship, a one team city and a game being televised) Elland Road is what you call an old-fashioned and traditional football ground. It cannot be described as stunning and certainly not modern compared to the likes of the recently built Tottenham Hotspur Stadium. You would say it has a great personality. To me it is beautiful, like a meat and potato pie at half-time. It has both a hostility and energy with a volume and an atmosphere like no other. Just at the moment the crowd bellowed out "Leeds, Leeds, Leeds" I honestly, sensed something in the air. The hairs stood up on the back of my neck. It felt like the Champions league game against AC Milan nearly 18 years ago. Optimism was oozing all around the ground. The crowd felt it, they sang, they became louder and louder, flags and scarves waved above their heads in unison with their Leeds United comrades beside them. Right then on that day at 16:30, the journey began.

The result that day delivered a triumphant 3–1 Leeds victory. After the match Marcelo Bielsa told BBC Radio Leeds, via a now permanent interpreter, "It's too soon to make any analysis either positive or negative. It was a game with high intensity, our players were very ambitious and they put in a great physical effort. The physical effort pleased me. The productivity was very high. We had the hope and the ambition to win. We have a dynamic team, an offensive team. We took risks when we were moving the ball." From that moment, from that result from that man, it confirmed the start of the 'United Revolución'.

Inspired, I began to photograph Elland Road, the fans and the city; United with their team, believing again in their club. I felt it and I hoped many more supporters did too. This book through the images and wonderfully written essays, contributed by passionate Leeds fans and professional writers hopes to capture this time. Like many sitting in the sunshine that game day I felt it has been a long time coming and although history and football is forever evolving this has been a glory time again.

This book is a document about a time between 2018–2020 and about Elland Road, Leeds United and their supporters; the love for their team again while the flame burns bright again, even if only for a short time.

JUSTIN SLEE
PHOTOGRAPHER

Clipper
www.clippergroup.co.uk
Clipper
Premier METALS WWW.PREMIER-METALS.CO.UK
Ladbrokes

olved
Clipper
www.clippergroup.co.uk
Clipper
Clipper
Global
globalautocare.co.uk
Global
CORPORATE VEHIC

"In terms of atmosphere, I would say the best I've heard it was during the play off semi-final against Derby. Even though we lost the match it was just so incredible before and during the game. Elland Road, when it's a full house is just unbelievable. Standing in the ground moments before games, is just something else. I've been to and played at many grounds around the world but that night before that game, standing in the tunnel was the most unique and memorable experience I've ever had."

Stuart Dallas

ALAW·MOT·

LUFC

"Supporting my team as a boy means I understand and I totally get the club and what being a fan of Leeds United means. Obviously, then playing for my club was my childhood dream. To then go on and win promotion as Captain was massive. A real lifetime memory, a dream and a Hollywood movie storyline, all rolled in to one.

As individual players and as a team we all worked incredibly hard to achieve our goals. We did it for the manager, our supporters, teammates and for ourselves. Coming back stronger from all the disappointments together. I guess that's why it meant so much and why we partied so hard that night in the stadium when we finally achieved promotion.

We had to celebrate with those fans outside the stadium to say thank you. You believed in us and supported us through the tough times and this time we all finally delivered.

For those supporters who could not be with us in that famous stadium during those moments it was tough. That is why we had to party hard for them. Sharing those moments on social media over our phones, for all those people stood outside the stadium and in their homes. It was all so typical Leeds too, unique, special, emotional and mental all at the same time.

A time truly unforgettable and hopefully we can achieve much, much more and show the Premier League the real 'Elland Road experience' in the not too distant future."

Liam Cooper

Year Formed (Leeds City)	**1904**
Year Formed (Leeds United)	**1919**
Elected to the Football League	**1920**

LEEDS UNITED

WEST STAND

LEEDS UNITED DESERVED A HERO

Dave Best

When I was a kid our club was full of heroes. My first proper memories of Leeds United are of Sgt Wilko's Barmy Army; that amazing early-nineties team who managed to win promotion from the old Second Division, then go on to finish top of the First Division just one year later.

I remember my dad driving me to Elland Road to watch Strachan, Speed, McAllister and Batty train on the old training ground just outside the West Stand. I waited, autograph book in hand, to meet my heroes and they (with the exception of Jon Newsome, who for some reason stormed straight through the crowd with a face like a smacked arse and into the stadium. I never forgave him...) took the time to sign every child's book. This was, blissfully for the players, I'm sure, way before the invention of the selfie, but my Dad managed to snap a photo of an awestruck David Best, dressed in a blue and yellow Leeds tracksuit, getting Gary Speed's autograph on his wind-up camera; a photo I found probably twenty years later, whilst cleaning out my old bedroom drawer, around the same time the world sadly lost him.

I had a season ticket at Elland Road with my dad from 1992 (I loved my Admiral away kit: in blue with an oh-so-nineties abrasive flash of pixilated yellow peppering on the side) until 2001 (Nike and Strongbow, need I say more!). We first got our tickets after the reconstruction of the East Stand, which aimed to fill it's 17,000 new seats through a scheme that offered two free children's season tickets if you bought one adult one. My brother and me also got a voucher book to spend in the stadium each match day. The only problem being that it cost two vouchers to get one sweaty burger at half-time, so by Christmas we had always emptied our book. That first half of the season full of cheap, non-descript meatiness was well worth it, though.

Every home game, as our dads headed to the bar, our gang of friends would all meet on the stairwell that led from the East Stand lower, to the East Stand upper and play a mini match with a crushed Coke can. When one of us would perform an expertly timed tackle we would sing, "You'll never pass Dorigo!" a homage to our stoic, engine of a left back. Every time someone lined up a shot from an audacious distance we would scream "SHOOOT BATTY!" a sarcastic chant derived from our blonde midfield local-lad's pathological resistance to shooting at goal.

Of course, as the years went by, I would eventually prefer to join my dad at the bar for his pre-match, mid-match and post-match pints, solving an infuriating riddle that had always eluded me as a child... *"Why does dad always need a wee ten minutes into the game?"* I grew up at Elland Road. It was my playground and my church, where every other weekend I would come and worship. Over those years, and still to this day, its magic hasn't dwindled. Every time I walk into the stadium I feel the same tingle down my spine I did when I first walked out into an all-standing Kop as a seven-year-old. The hum of concentrated humanity all poised toward a similar goal; kids in replica shirts, scarves and hats, staring at the pitch wide-eyed and in total awe; old guys chuckling and discussing tactics; obsessive fans sat elusive, reading their programme with a pained intensity.

I was one of the lucky ones. I was a child through relatively bountiful harvests at Elland Road. Sure, the George Graham era was somewhat of a damp squib, filled with countless goalless draws and bland football, but compared with what was to come it was a flipping pleasure cruise! Heroes came and heroes went (or didn't in some cases). Tony Yeboah's thunderbolt of a right foot (that Liverpool game was the only one I missed that year, due to being on holiday. Damn Eurocamp!), Gary Kelly's speed and productivity, Jimmy Floyd Hasselbaink's expert finishing (and subsequent half-arsed cartwheels), Ian Harte's wand of a left foot, Alan Smith's local-boy grit and heart, Lucas Radebe's leadership and loyalty, Bowyer's late runs into the box, Viduka's four sublime goals against Liverpool (what a gorgeous game that was. A proper 'I was there' moment!) All culminating in a Champion's League run in the 2000/01 Season that even now I barely believe happened. I saw my club hold pace with the best in the world. Real Madrid, Inter Milan, Barcelona and Lazio all graced our sacred pitch and attending those games was a great privilege that was not lost on me, even then. It felt like I was at the perfect age to enjoy those wonderful European nights. I'd go with my dad to the home games and join my friends in the local pub for the away games, all in the year before I left my hometown for University. It was like the longest, most amazing leaving party ever.

Then… stuff happened.

My youth left and it took my football club with it. Suddenly I was an adult, sucker-punched with the reality of having to live in Middlesbrough for three years, and my club just sank. And sank. And sank! I'll whizz through it, because, we all know the story and, well… it's not too fun to write about. It goes something like this:

Blah, blah, Ridsdale, spend, spend, spend, blah, overly expensive goldfish bowl, blah, sell, sell, sell, blah, and relegation! Man United fans laughing at me in the Student Union, blah, blah, losing in the playoffs, blah, blah administration, blah, blah, League Frigging One! Blah, blah, fifteen points deduction, and Bates Out! Dennis Wise, blah, blah, losing in the playoffs, then again in the final, blah, sitting on my tour bus miserable on the way home from Wembley, blah, blah, blah, Grayson! Ray of light! Promotion! Beckford! Just missing out of playoffs! False dawn, blah, blah, blah, GFH, blah, blah, criminals, blah, blah, Cellino, blah, "This guy's a mentalist!" blah, blah, lots of rubbish, Italians, blah, blah, Dave Hockaday??? Blah, despair, resignation, chaos, and laughingstock, BLAH BLAH BLAH!!!

You could count the heroes during our fifteen-year holiday-in-hades on one hand. Jermaine Beckford, for his goal against Man United in the FA Cup, his goals in general and subsequent promotion-securing goal at home to Bristol Rovers. Simon Grayson, for collecting us at our lowest ebb and with an actually eye-catching brand of football, managing us out of League One. Erm… Andy Hughes, for his passion and versatility during that hard-fought promotion season. Erm… erm… McCormack for one Championship season? Maybe?

And then, it happened.

No one really knew what to make of Andrea Radrizzani. An Italian businessman with zero experience of Championship football. Massimo Cellino, that guitar wielding, manager munching lunatic had pretty much scarred us for life when it came to Italian owners. Radrizzani had hired Victor Orta as Director of football, the man who was driven out of Middlesbrough by a braying fan-base who thought he was the worst thing to happen to their club since Juninho left. It all felt a little bit like another chapter in the ever-growing anthology of doom that was modern day Leeds United.

It was all going to script. Our manager, Garry Monk, jumped ship two days after Radrizzani's takeover and was replaced by Thomas Christiansen, an ex-Spanish international with very little managing pedigree. He was, after a decent start, inevitably rubbish and got sacked for the Barnsley manager Paul Heckingbottom, who historically hated Leeds United and went about managing them as if he still did. It got to the point where I was watching Heckingbottom's team thinking, "There's no discernible tactics here at all. He's just putting eleven players on the pitch and hoping that it works. I swear there's no point even having team managers at this point... at this level they don't seem to be able to have any impact on what happens on the pitch."

I was wrong. Oh, I was so very, very, wrong.

I'm not going to lie. I knew nothing about the man. He'd managed Chile and Argentina. Okay, he's been around a bit. His nickname is 'El Loco'? I see, another shot in the dark. Another loose cannon. Another comedy-of-errors in the making...

Oh, I was so very, very, very, wrong!

At the end of Marcelo Bielsa's first Championship game against Stoke City in August 2018 I was gobsmacked. Dumbfounded. What had I just watched? Marauding full-backs, Liam Cooper spraying passes left and right, some mediocre kid called Kalvin Phillips, who had previously looked like he was destined for a career in the lower leagues, playing like a seasoned quarterback, crunching tackles and starting attacks at will. Pablo Hernandez appearing to have the ball on a string, Mateusz Klich ("wait, isn't he that random Polish guy we keep sending on loan?") running around like he's had six bags of Skittles, linking the play exquisitely; It was like the whole team had angel dust sprinkled over their heads and they no longer resembled anything like their former selves. It was magic.

All season Leeds played above themselves, rarely leaving the top two. Fans flocked. Fans believed. Fans saw a future that was bright, as opposed to an empty black hole of uncertainty. Bielsa demanded upgrades of the training facilities, he obsessively controlled player's diets, and he drilled them within an inch of their lives. His exhausting training sessions, carving each and every single player into an Adonis in a matter of months. The football was joyful; it was sexy, and more mesmerising than it had been in well over a decade. I remember the home game against West Brom that year.

I went with my dad. We sat in the East Stand upper and watched a full-to-the rafters Elland Road nearly explode when, after sixteen seconds, Pablo Hernandez curled a peach into the top corner in front of the South Stand. The noise... the elation... it took us right back to those glory nights almost twenty years ago. There was no doubt in either of our minds: our Leeds United was back.

The playoff semi-final defeat against Derby at the end of that year was painful. It was wrong on so many levels (up yours, Frank Lampard!) but I knew if we kept Bielsa at the helm, we would go again the next year stronger, wiser and with more belief. There was no stopping what had begun in LS11. And so, it was... in the 19/20 Season, blighted by a Pandemic, which meant that we couldn't even be there at the church when it happened. We won the Championship by a comfortable margin and returned to the Premier League as Champions.

A new generation got its heroes. Pablo the wizard, with his last gasp goal against Swansea. Kalvin Phillips brave, passionate performances in front of the back four. Liam Cooper defying the early criticism to be the leader we all needed. And Bielsa, Bielsa, Bielsa. That honest, earnest, humble, kind, scary, obsessive deity of a man who steps off the team bus armed with keyrings and hugs to give to adoring kids as they wait to catch a glimpse of him. He, for whom no statue at Elland Road would be big enough. The Argentine has performed lifesaving surgery on this club that will hold for years and years to come.

It's a great time to be a Leeds fan. Could do with them bringing back the burger vouchers though.

Dave Best —
Bass player in the platinum-selling Leeds band, *The Pigeon Detectives*. Also held a music and culture column in the *Yorkshire Evening Post*.

THE FIVES
5
FAMOUS FIVES
STRENGTH IN NUMBERS
THE SEVENS
7
MAGNIFICENT SEVENS
STRENGTH IN NUMBERS
ENTRANCE
9

ENTRANCE 15
MARCHING ON TOGETHER
Welcome to Elland Road
In case of abandonment, please retain tickets.
ENTRANCE
15
TURNSTILE
91 & 92
92
91

WELCOME TO
ELLAND ROAD
#TheOnlyPlaceForUs
LEEDS

"ELLAND ROAD IS THE MOST INTIMIDATING VENUE IN EUROPE"

Alex Ferguson

Centenary
Pavilion
Car Park
Matchday
West Stand
VIP Parking

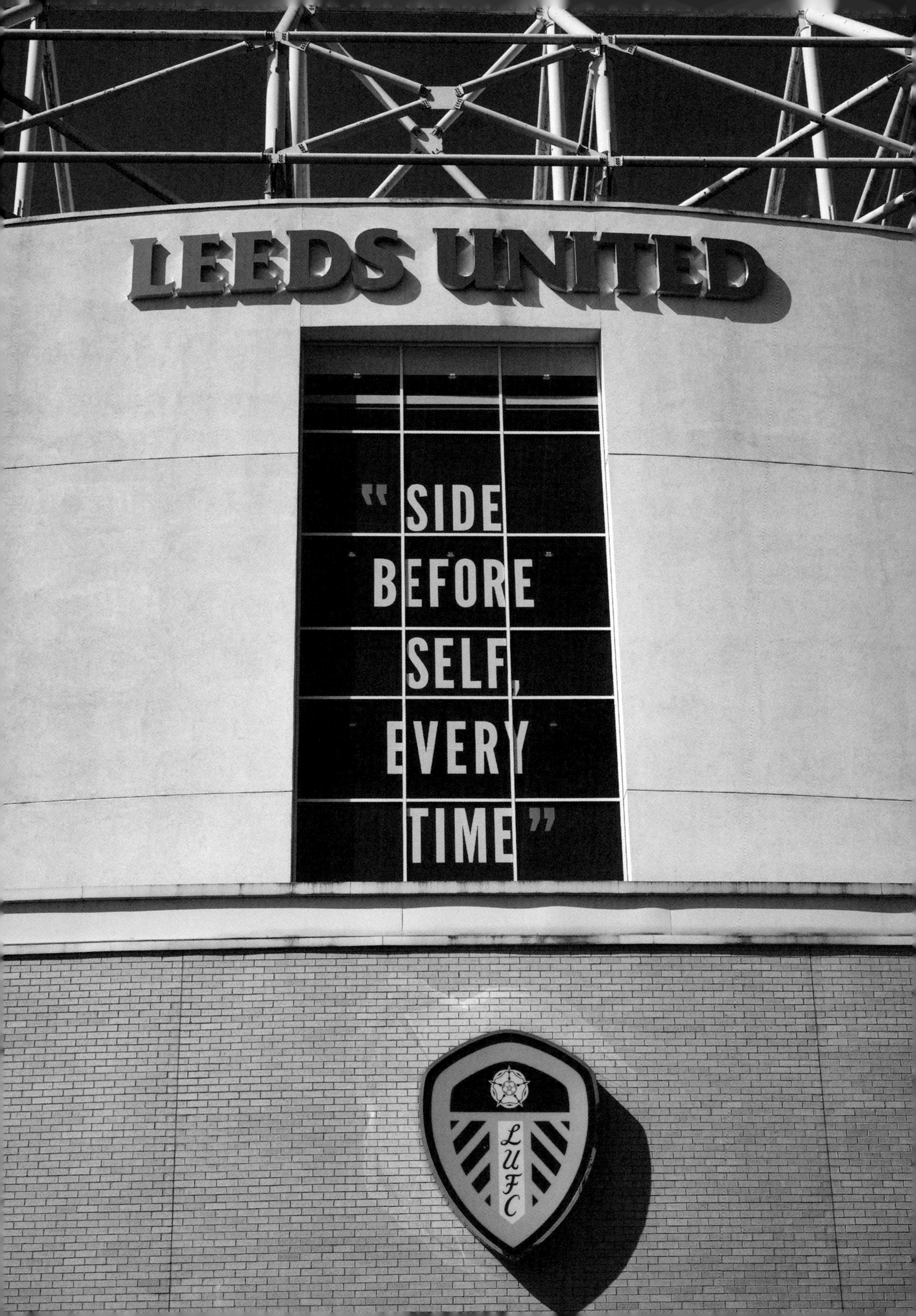
LEEDS UNITED
"SIDE BEFORE SELF, EVERY TIME"
LUFC

Clipper
www.clippergroup.co.
M.A.M.O
Britcab

"There will come a day when stadiums like Elland Road disappear from the landscape because English football is forever moving towards the new and the shiny but if you want to understand Leeds United, you only need to experience their surroundings: raw, rough, aggressive and devoted. It's smaller than Anfield, Old Trafford and other grounds but there's something different about it. Something more visceral. When I think of the noise, I always think of Luciano Becchio's goal against Millwall and the deafening mayhem as fans spilling into the press box. Bottle that and sell it for a fortune."

Phil Hay

53°46'40"N
1°34'20"W

Capacity	**37,890**
Record Attendance	**57,892**
Vs Sunderland FA Cup 5th Round Replay, 15th March 1967	
Best Home Unbeaten Streak	**39**
4th May 1968 – 28th March 1970	

THE LEEDS UNITED
Kappa
Kappa

Kappa
PERSONALISE IT!
PERSONALISE IT! IN STORE TODAY
ANY NAME 9
LETTERS £1
SHIRT NUMBERS £4
SHORT NUMBERS £2.50
EFL £7
PERSONALISE IT! IN STORE TODAY
ANY NAME 9

"I always enjoyed playing at Elland Road and being a Leeds lad it always felt a bit special.

I was lucky to play with some great players, but just being around Billy Bremner when I was starting out was extra special. I suppose one of my biggest memories of Elland Road was seeing the place erupt when I scored at the 'Kop End' against Man City. The noise was incredible, you would have thought we'd just won the FA Cup!"

David Batty

"YOU GET NOWT FOR BEING SECOND"
DON REVIE

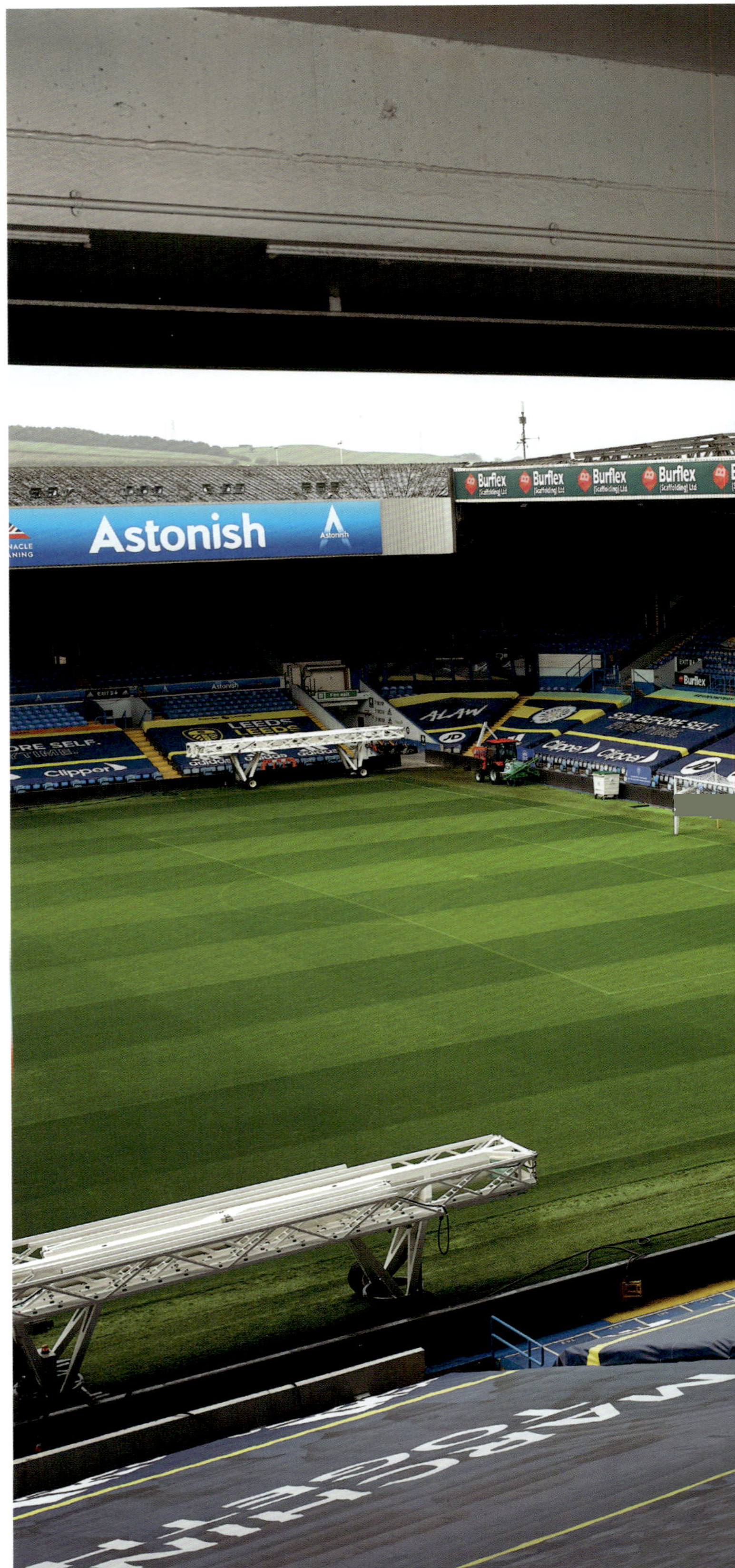

Burflex
(Scaffolding) Ltd
ALAW
SIDE BEFORE SELF.
EVERYTIME.
SBOTOP
UNTIL THE WORLD STOPS GOING ROUND.
LEEDS
EXIT

FOREVER & EVER, WE'LL FOLLOW OUR TEAM

Heidi Haigh

I have supported Leeds United for over 50 years and I am privileged to have witnessed them becoming one of the best sides in Europe. In my early days at the start of the 1970s I followed the team everywhere, and for seven years I did not miss a game. My early hero was Billy Bremner, a pivotal member of that great Don Revie's team. That period instilled my lifetime love and loyalty of supporting my club.

As a young woman, due to that fantastic Leeds team and their achievements on the pitch, I was able to travel to Europe. I visited Salonika, Greece for the European Cup Winners' Cup Final in 1973 and Paris, for the unforgettable European Cup Final in 1975. That same year I also went to Zurich, Anderlecht and Barcelona. The team showed me the way and encouraged me and gave me the confidence for adventure. They provided me with so much more than football. In those early days I helped build and cement the support for Leeds United to the football World.

Under Manager Howard Wilkinson, in the early nineties, was another great time to be a fan. The intense atmosphere on the terraces inside Elland Road returned and was electrifying. The crowd became the twelfth man, creating extra energy in the players and driving the team forward. If the opposition scored the supporters would immediately increase the intensity, inspire and back the team. I have been very lucky to witness all of the clubs successful periods, including the start of the Millennium, which promised so much, but sadly did not quite deliver under David O'Leary and his talented young team. I guess we all know the sorry story from then.

During the in-between years of success, things became so bad on and off the pitch. Starting, for me, with the Leeds 70s side being broken up. For many years it could become a real chore to follow the team and my loyalty was tested many times and to the limits. What always kept me believing was the fantastic camaraderie. Friendships I made in those early years stayed with me and became my football family. Many connections that I made are still there to this day and that is what I love the most about our fans. Reminiscing the good times, laughing at the not so good times on and off the pitch. 'Ups and Downs' we follow our team. Sharing those moments helps you realise how good the young fans have it again, right now.

When Marcelo Bielsa was first appointed manager of Leeds United (I'm old school, and I don't call him coach) I had never heard of him. I began to research. The first thing I discovered was that he walked out of a previous club (Lazio 2016) after just two days. A bit worrying even by Brian Clough's standard of just 44 days as our manager in 1974. I took a step back and looked at the bigger picture. The more I discovered the more I liked. He reminded me of Don with his meticulous team preparation. Bielsa also immaculately prepared. I read of him watching videos of all our previous league games as well as the oppositions. I believed we were going to be in good hands again.

From my team all I ever ask is to see is the players giving 100%. Working hard and never giving up the fight, until the final whistle. I insist they display a pride in the club, its history and in wearing the famous white shirt. Being totally honest, I don't think I ever imagined that Bielsa could transform the side he inherited into the team that we see today. We have played some fantastic football with incredible individual player improvements. The playing style and the passing makes me reminisce about past glory years. Attacking with energy and with great teamwork. Playing with a no-fear approach. Although, playing out from the back does, with all its tactical benefits, sometimes have my head in my hands. The team may be calm and collected but my heart has missed many a beat.

As a home and away season ticket holder I have been lucky enough to be at many games. Nowadays, my eyes are also for the fans. My experiences are shared through my own photographs and words posted on my online blog 'Follow Leeds United and Me.' I enjoy sharing my experiences and celebrating with the fellow fans and it gives me real added joy with a feeling of togetherness. Like life, the unpredictability of being a Leeds United fan goes hand in hand. After the disappointment at the end of the 2018/19 season and the words of 'Leeds, Leeds are falling apart, again.' ringing in my ears I wrote in my journal. "2019, Leeds United will be promoted, in their Centenary year!" This was our time. Marcelo, his staff and the team had brought the fans' belief back.

The following season, on the pitch and emotionally, was certainly not an easy ride. I just kept trying to be positive and saying "we can do it", with many around me losing the faith. "Aim for the top, keep fighting and get as many points as possible and let's see where we end up" became my words of encouragement.

Just as the team were on an amazing run of results, the Coronavirus pandemic hit the whole country. On the 13th March 2020 the Premier League, EFL and WSL were all suspended indefinitely, putting a halt to the whole season and potentially all our dreams. Promotion to the Premier League with nine games of the season remaining was so close. Many results-based equations and possible league outcomes were bounced around. The wait was unbearable.

Forward three months, June 2020. Football restart, here we go again and the fear of the season being cancelled is now over. It is replaced with the doubt again. Can we get over the line? Will the team have the fitness still for the high press? Doubts intensified, pressure increased and especially after the disappointing first game back; an away defeat to Cardiff City.

However, this time the 'Ups' prevailed over the 'Downs.' This was going to be our time! After 16 years, the team delivered and in style. Winning seven games and drawing one of the final eight games.

It was fantastic, joyous, although mixed with a little disappointment at not being able to attend any of those remaining games in person. The virus meant all the games had to played behind closed doors and in empty stadiums. Void of spectators, with the exception of 15,000 cardboard cut outs inside Elland Road. In all my years as a fan that was very tough. I was so desperate to get back and support my team. I found it torturous watching from afar, I was kicking every ball as if I was still there. During the home fixture against Barnsley with the team under pressure and clinging on to a 1–0 lead, the last 30 minutes seemed an eternity. I was so desperate for the win and as soon as the final whistle blew with Leeds hanging on, I burst into tears; the relief that we had got the win just overcame me.

The next couple of days saw Leeds United's promotion confirmed to the Premier League and followed by being crowned 'Champions' of the Championship. We even squeezed in a guard of honour at Derby County on the way. It was amazing watching those moments on television and seeing the fans outside the ground. Celebrating with the team, live on social media. The journey had ended. For me this final moment was tinged with a little sadness. Something had been taken away from us. Not being inside the ground, cheering and celebrating the moment with the team, all together was very hard.

Being a Leeds supporter for me is about the togetherness. The players come and go but the one thing that will always remain is the fantastic loyalty and our love of Leeds United. I can't wait to be back at Elland Road, amongst them.

LUFC, Marching on Together!

Heidi Haigh —
Curator of the blog, *Follow Me and Leeds United*, and Author of *Once a Leeds fan, always a Leeds fan* and *Leeds are going to the Premier League!*

THE OLD PEACOCK
REAL ALE HOUSE & KITCHEN
Yorkshire Life & Living North VOTED IN THE TOP 10 CURRY HOUSES IN YORKSHIRE
sky sports football

HOME
Billy's
SPORTS BAR
1961 -1980 HIGHLIGHTS
1964
1965
1967
1968

DIRTY LEEDS
AND PROUD
ALL SCARVES £6.00 Each
LEEDS
BILLY BREMNER
KEMAR ROOFE

"There is always doubt and always fear. There is always trouble, always tension. Tension and trouble; fear and doubt; war, war, war and then, right on cue as if by magic, here come Leeds, Leeds, Leeds."

David Peace, *The Damned United*

MARCHING ON TOGETHER
Coca-Cola
Coca-Cola
epay
cash
CAFE
LEEDS

DIRTY LEEDS

"My greatest memory of Elland Road as a player has to be my first game. My debut; I was 17 years of age. It was New Year's Day 1966 against Sheffield Wednesday. A good day, especially for a Scotsman. We won 3–0, and I happened to score. I hit one 25 yards out into the goal at the Kop end. They were the days of standing in the Kop and I was very young so for me it was a real stand-out game.

I played in some wonderful matches, some big, big games, including big European nights. I also enjoyed watching some top European teams visit during Champions League nights alongside David O'Leary. But for me that game against Sheffield Wednesday, was a real stand-out personal moment. The atmosphere in the ground was always terrific when I played. I played in a very good team, but I have to say that for Marcelo Bielsa's team playing in the Championship, the atmosphere was also terrific – as good as I have ever known at Elland Road. That was a credit to the players and how they were playing. The way Marcelo got the players to play and the brand of football being played was really good. When I played, because we were a top team, the atmosphere was always great but it was nice to see it return to the same level I had played under again. Everyone in the town is buzzing. The fans going to the games are really up for it and that is why it was such a shame about the fans not being allowed in during the pandemic. Hopefully it will return and we can ride any blips in the road and get those days to return quickly.

In my time Don ran the football club. Bielsa has been the same and what he says goes. Top managers are all their own men. I would say Bielsa is very similar to Don. He is a bit of a throw-back to the old days like that. Especially regarding the football. On the playing side, what he says goes and everyone knows that. We always thought Don was ahead of his time looking at teams, with his dossiers and game preparation. Bielsa is also like that with the way he prepares his teams for games. They do not just train just for training's sake. They prepare for the games. Would I have liked to play under Bielsa? I do not know, things have changed. He does not get to close to the players, but he respects them and the players respect him. The players have bought into his ideas. What he does get, too, is the fans. He respects them and he understands them. He has bought into the city of Leeds and the passion the fans have for their football club. This was all brought to the fore when they won the Championship."

Eddie Gray

UNITED A.F.C.
LTD.
PADDOCK
MEMBER'S TICKET
Not Transferable
Season

CAFE
SANDWICH BAR
FISH
&
CHIPS
Litter
OPEN
DBH
73

“Stand out moments has to be when me and my son Hari sat in the South Stand against Cardiff. This was Hari’s first time in the South Stand and within 5 minutes of kick off he turned to me and said, ‘Daddy, what’s a sheep shagger?’ I replied, ‘you need to ask your mum when we get home’ – We spent the rest of the game on our feet singing.

Secondly, meeting Marcelo Bielsa in the flesh! What an amazing man with an incredible aura. Getting to actually speak to the man responsible for us achieving promotion was unbelievable. I was absolutely star-struck; even the Mrs said that I’ve never looked at her the way I did Bielsa.”

Chaz Singh (@Punjabi_whites)

MARCHING ON TOGETHER
ELLAND ROAD NEWS
CHICOS

HISTORY, REPEATING MYSELF

Robert Endeacott

'You are my sunshine, my only sunshine,
You make me happy, when skies are grey,
You never notice, how much I love you,
Please don't take my sunshine away.'

... a snippet of the song from absolutely yonks ago (the 1930s), made better in Leeds in the 70s.

We sang it with gusto at Elland Road, adding in some timely clapping as well. It was always one of my favourite chants, sung by faithful vocalists around our football ground standing on the Gelderd, Lowfields and South Stand terraces. This is obviously well before Elland Road became all-seater. I am rubbish at remembering song lyrics and there's more proof of it here: I always used to sing – *You'll never know* ***Leeds****, how much I love you,* ***'til you*** *take my sunshine away.* My heart was always in the right place, even if some words weren't!

Leeds songs conjure up images in my mind as soon as I'm reminded of them, that's why I'm rambling down another memory lane here, it seems fitting for this book. My better half enjoys taking the mick out of me by saying that Elland Road is like a second home to me. Not so much this year of course, due to the 2020 'Pandemia', but it's normally a favourite dig of hers. I think she underestimates how common this sort of feeling with the football ground is amongst Leeds supporters. There are countless people who have been to Elland Road and been to more matches than me, and who probably feel more sentimental about the place as well. Anyway, she's wrong, it's actually more like my third home.

I was lucky in many respects that my dear old dad Barry worked at Elland Road as one of the ground staff, from around 1970 until 1996, so I had many opportunities to view the stadium's interior and underbelly, so to speak, that many won't have. It could hardly be described as a secret entry into the inner sanctum of the workings of Leeds United AFC but it was always exciting and I did feel kind of privileged.

I was always very shy as a kid but my dad helped me overcome this insecurity to some degree by introducing me to a new hobby, that of autograph collecting. Consequently, on Elland Road match days I could often be seen loitering with intent after – sometimes before – games, waiting with my pen and book to pounce on the famous and not too unsuspecting targets. Dad had work to do before matches kicked off (three o'clock on a Saturday, seventhirty for night matches) on the pitch and around the player dressing rooms so I just had to hang around the vicinity really. I developed enough confidence to firmly and politely ask for autographs from my Leeds heroes as well as any anti-heroes from the away teams. I even plucked up enough courage to ask Sean Connery *twice* for his signature, he was there for Jack Charlton's testimonial against Celtic in 1973.

Oddly enough, I never got Brian Clough's signature. The one chance I had was when he was Leeds boss and was just coming out of the players' dressing room. As I was waiting directly outside the door, he looked down at me with my proffered autograph book and replied that he didn't have enough time to sign it. I suddenly felt like Oliver Twist asking for more, though he was perfectly civil with me to be fair to him. He spent more time apologising than it would have taken him to do it, *and* he ruffled my hair too. He wasn't in poor spirits so I suspect it was immediately after his only win as Leeds manager. It's probably the one single thing he did while he was our manager that I forgive him for!

As my Dad's employment started when Don Revie's team was at their best (the first 'phase' at least), as reigning champions for the first time, so did my being an avid fan. I never felt like I was better or more loyal than anyone else or that I was a 'superfan' (which probably wasn't even a word in those days), just that I was a super-lucky-fan! I have absolutely no idea what my first match was or what the score-line was. In truth, I only managed to see the briefest of glimpses of matches from the Lowfields Road side in those early days. Even as a four or five year-old, kids weren't allowed to sit on the Lowfields pitch side wall, so that effectively was that. Eventually things improved as Dad got me into the West Stand.

As a child, the pain of a Leeds defeat was always sharp and unforgettable, the immediate aftermaths miserable. By far the worst case was 1975 (just stating the year is enough for people to know which match I mean), I never thought I could ever feel as bad again about a Leeds result as that night, but subsequent semi-final defeats and The Unthinkable of relegation in 1982 certainly took me bloody close. In fact, most of the 1980s dragged my spirits down to depressed levels! I suppose the eighties were my formative years, the sort of times when events around you could cause you to either sink or swim. I was undoubtedly sinking in 1982 thanks to the team being really poor, especially on the night we were all but relegated after nearly twenty years in the top flight. My plight wasn't helped by my stupid decision to hitchhike to the match in question, West Bromwich Albion there and back, or the jay-walking charge later on when dropped off at Hartshead Moor services back in West Yorkshire. Defeats still hurt now of course, and I'm not ashamed to admit that football, which is 'only a game' don't forget, remains a personal priority even with other responsibilities and worries in life to consider. I *know* we have just spent 16 years outside the top division and it has hurt and been very stressful for us all but I honestly felt more downhearted and desperate from 1982 to 89. 1987s heroics by Billy Bremner's team – which ultimately ended in failure – caused the yearning for success and promotion to be even starker.

I remember actually being with my dad when John Reynolds informed him he'd got the job he'd applied for, around 1969 or 70. Cec Burroughs and Ray Hardy were still at Elland Road when Dad joined their workforce, and they were always kind to us, too. John though would soon become his immediate boss, and he proved to be one of the finest fellas of Elland Road history. Dad suffered many significant challenges in his life and I make no apologies for getting emotional when I think about his struggles, but I know he enjoyed working under John for those twenty-plus years, even when the club was in decline for a large part of the duration. It's easy to understand why. I always think of John's attitude and man-management style as like that of Don Revie's: everyone *mattered*, regardless of job or status, and he *cared*. From 1961, Leeds under The Don (and chairman Harry Reynolds, no relation to John) was built on family, loyalty and dedication to the United cause. I'm not as closely attached to the club these days, though I've written a bit and done some 'decorating' in the East Stand (with a couple of mates) where my season ticket seat resides but I do get the feeling that the good times are with us again at Elland Road and Thorp Arch. *Keep Fighting* and *Side Before Self Every* Time are working wonders, even in these generally crap and gloomy times.

Don Revie's career as Leeds boss commenced when the club was at a worryingly low ebb, toiling in Division Two and with the third beckoning them. Whilst it probably took longer than the fans wanted, Harry Reynolds (soon to be the new Leeds chairman) thankfully, was a patient man with staunch faith in the young manager. Reynolds was a very astute man, highly successful in business, but there is a feeling even he was at times in awe of Revie's planning and forward thinking. Revie brought in new ideas and approaches relative to players' diet and training, and he insisted that *standards* were markedly improved across the club. He took full advantage of skills and expertise available from coaching staff there, unassuming but brilliant men such as Les Cocker, Syd Owen, Maurice Lindley, Cyril Partridge and Bob English, as well as the already-in-place scouting network, one of the club's real assets at the time.

I have always believed that Leeds United would have been nothing had Revie not taken over, and the man who entrusted the job to him therefore deserves great praise too. Attention to detail was always a priority for Revie and his coaching staff, essential for not only assessing his own players – current and potential – but also to highlight the strengths and weaknesses of opposing teams. This is where the famous dossiers came in, signifying excellent, in-depth analyses of the opposition. Such meticulous methods helped Leeds United develop into one of the best teams in the world. Does anyone recognise similar qualities at the club nowadays?

Now of course we are privileged to have Marcelo Bielsa in charge. Thanks to Bielsa and his crew (and credit where it's due, to Radrizzani, Kinnear and Orta for bringing them in) the club is on the cusp of something fantastic and special, I really believe it. They have already achieved something pretty damned spectacular, champions of the Championship, and now they're making their mark on the Premier League with real style. It continues to be a bloody awful time but Bielsa's Leeds are at least brightening it up. The quality of football our team is playing is genuinely bloomin' special, creating beautiful shockwaves around the sports world. I honestly doubt that many Leeds fans are too surprised at how well the team has fared so far in the Premier League, certain signs have been there since he took over. Leeds fans have always wanted/demanded passionate intensity and commitment from the players, and that's exactly what we are seeing, with sparkling individual and team performances added in. The improvements are astounding, they really are, I don't think I'm exaggerating!

When the inevitable happens and Bielsa leaves us (I KNOW, I don't want to think about it either!) I just hope that whoever is in charge at the club will have learned from the shocking past

MATCHDAY TICKET COLLECTIONS ONLY
OUT
IN

and accept that some form of 'continuity' is infinitely is better than recruiting an outspoken bull in a china shop (whose autograph I never managed to get.)

I hope no one reading my comparisons of The Don and 'El Loco' thinks I'm being arrogant or wise after the event. In case there are any such misgivings, I should say that two years ago I sent a copy of my John Charles novel 'The Gigante' to Mr Bielsa, with a personal letter telling him how much he reminded me of Mr Revie. I was chuffed but not surprised to receive a reply, thanking me for the comments and also telling me that he would read the book when his English was good enough. More importantly, he signed the letter!

M.O.T!

Robert Endeacott —
Author of the Novels, *One Northern Soul, No More Heroes, Dirty Leeds, After Extra Time,* and *The Gigante.*

LEEDS · LEEDS
SUPER LEEDS
EDS · LEEDS

HERE WE GO WITH LEEDS UNITED
WE'RE GONNA GIVE THE BOYS A HAND
STAND UP & SING FOR LEEDS UNITED
THEY ARE THE GREATEST IN THE LAND

BRANDON
CDs £7.99 each
2 for £13.98
THANK YOU!

WELCOME TO
ELLAND ROAD
#TheOnlyPlaceForUs
JESUS
CHRIST
CAME INTO THIS WORLD
TO SAVE SINNERS
REPENT

WE'VE HAD OUR UPS

& DOWNS

HOMES
70-80-90-2000's
60p EACH
70-80-90-2000's
80p EACH
3 · £2 · 66p EACH
8 · £5 · 62½p EACH
17 · £10 · 58p EACH
WHITE AND BLUE!
LEEDS UNITED
LEEDS
v Arsenal
LUFC
UEFA CUP
Leeds United FC v Grasshopper C. Z.

MARCHING ON TOGETHER
PRIDE OF YORKSHIRE
THE PRIDE OF YORKSHIRE
CLUB AND COUNTRY
ELLAND ROAD
ST. GEORGE'S DAY
23rd APRIL
ENGLAND
NORTHERN SOUL
ALL NIGHT
UP ALL
KEEP THE FAITH

"Having being fortunate enough to have played for Leeds, I have always stated that the best times for me with the club were as a fan. Why? I think it is a cultural thing. I am from Leeds, and a proud Yorkshireman as was my dad who was also a very keen sportsman and supporter. Standing on the kop was the greatest thrill, and my mum even preferred to stand there when I was a player. I was the only player exchanging West Stand seat-tickets for Kop tickets on matchdays!

I was spoiled as a child being able to go down to Elland Road to see the great Leeds United side of the late 60s early 70s. Every player in that era is a hero to me. That side will never be equalled in terms of their ability, success and more importantly the positive influence they had to people all over the world. I also had the pleasure of meeting the great John Charles and Bobby Collins who led the way in terms of establishing Leeds United as one of the best sides in Europe (the world) has ever seen.

I was in the stands on 20th October 1973 Vs Liverpool (we won 1–0) when the pantomime horse ran on to the pitch. That really epitomised the fan culture and humour – as the horse was dragged away by the stewards, the fans started singing 'my horse,my horse, I was saying goodbye to my horse.'

As a young fan I loved the Leeds United (Trevillion) marketing at the time it was totally unique and brilliant. I loved the coordinated warm ups where the opposition just stared in awe, I loved the wave to the crowd before the match, and I still own a pair of no. 8 and no. 9 stocking tags! The yellow kit was my first ever football kit and I still love the smiley badge. I hate the current badge!!

I think as a player, one home game in particularly that stands out for me: 7th November 1981, my 20th birthday and my second full game for Leeds. I scored the winner in a 1–0 win in the First Division against Notts County. The fans started singing 'Happy Birthday' to me it was very humbling and thrilling."

Aiden Butterworth

THE FOOTBALL LEAGUE
CUP FINAL
ARSENAL v LEEDS UNITED
WEMBLEY
£5
DERBY COUNTY
£10
LEEDS UNITED v F.C. JUVENTUS
£12
£15
ANFIELD REVIEW
LEEDS UNITED
GLASGOW CELTIC
£7
OFFICIAL
£5
SEMI-FINAL
£3
Leeds United versus Chelsea
COUP D'EUROPE
F.C. ZURICH
£10
LEEDS UNITED
Ferencvaros
£8
estac
FINAL
£7
ARSENAL v LEEDS UNITED
FINAL
£8
LEEDS UNITED v SUNDERLAND
WEMBLEY STADIUM
Programa Oficial del F.C. BARCELONA
£40
£300
£100
F.C.Bayern/Leeds Munich United
£10
F.C.Bayern/Leeds Munich United
DERBY Play off To Clear £1 each
VALETTA F.C.
LEEDS UTD
£10
LEEDS UNITED
SUPPORTERS
£5
£5

kappa
LEEDS
32Red

"My stand out memory at Elland Road as a player without hesitation was on the 4th of April 2001. The game Deportivo La Coruna during the Champions League quarter-final first leg. Played under floodlights with a capacity crowd and an amazing atmosphere.

Twenty minutes into the game, we win a free-kick when their player manhandled Smudge (Alan Smith) to the floor. H (Harry Kewell) caused enough havoc in the wall to create an opening for me to smash home the free kick. A momentous goal for me one of my best and a memory that still feels like it was played out yesterday. The crowd erupted and the knee slide celebration in front of the Kop was not bad either.

Years later when I was playing for Levante in Spain the keeper I scored past that night, José Francisco Molina signed for Levante too. We chatted a lot about that game, the atmosphere and my free-kick."

Ian Harte

"Weirdly enough one of my lasting memories of Elland Road and what it means to be Leeds isn't from our victorious 92 team or our Champions League runs or even our resurgence under Bielsa, it comes from our dark times. I remember looking around the stadium and seeing everyone partying, celebrating, jumping up and down and generally 'going mental,' because we were just so terrible. Losing to really small clubs week in week out in League One and sometimes the atmosphere was still incredible. It was gallows humour but I remember thinking to myself 'this fan base is unique,' this isn't ordinary, quite the opposite."

Micky P Kerr

LEEDS UNITED
FOOTBALL CLUB STORE
KIT ON
ALWAYS
Logistics evolved

Dad

WELCOME TO
ELLAND ROAD
#TheOnlyPlaceForUs
ENTRANCE
13
32Red
YORKSHIRE
Evening
SINCE 1925

"Going to Elland Road is one of the great experiences in football. It's the sights and sounds, the sense of expectation, the excited chatter between friends and families, the feeling of a congregation gathering for worship. It's the fans queuing outside the chip shop, paying tribute to Billy Bremner by his statue, nodding respectfully to the Don Revie statue, going into the club shop. It's the rivers of humanity all flowing into the ground, all united by one passion: Leeds."

Henry Winter

49

MANAGING TO SUCCEED

COMPARING HOWARD WILKINSON & MARCELO BIELSA

Dave Simpson

"I really admire Bielsa because he dares to be different," Howard Wilkinson said at the start of the 2020/21 season, after the Leeds United manager had become the first to take the club back into the top flight of English football since Wilkinson himself back in 1990. "I suppose if he was a singer, he would be Frank Sinatra – he does it his way." As did "Sergeant Wilko." On the face of it, the two coaches – their Leeds United careers separated by two and a half decades – could not be more different.

Sheffield-born Wilkinson was the gruff, seemingly dour but drily humorous Yorkshireman who built on promotion to achieve the ultimate honour at Leeds. He remains the last English manager to win the league title (in 1991/92, the last season before the old First Division became the Premier League). Bielsa conducts his press conferences in analytical Argentinian. Wilko preferred a dry, combative Yorkshire accent. When the former [PE] schoolteacher was once asked "What did you teach?" he replied simply "children", bone dry humour which did not travel to the London press, who dubbed him a "smartarse" the next day.

The "Sergeant" – a former if unremarkable footballer who came up through the English game, from lowly Boston to Notts County, to then top flight Sheffield Wednesday and then to Leeds – coached in a different era, of fewer substitutes (only one until 1987, after which two were allowed), heavier balls and no back pass rule until the season after Wilkinson had won the league. Bielsa, born into a wealthy Argentine family was a studious child, inspired by his grandfather's collection of 30,000 books into avid reading. He built up his own vast collection of sports magazines in an early hint of the innovative, analytical approach to coaching that is now so revered by Pep Guardiola.

As a player, Bielsa made the Argentine First Division with Newell's Old Boys but retired to coach at 25. He has coached the Argentine and Chilean national teams and some of the world's great clubs – Athletic Bilbao, Marseille, Lazio and Lille – often short spells marked by controversies and political difficulties with the clubs' hierarchies. He won titles in Argentina with Newell's Old Boys (two) and Velez but a similar European honour eludes him. Before Leeds, Wilko had yet to win a league, having secured three minor cups with Boston and a promotion to the top flight with Wednesday. Two very different characters, two very different stories, but both needed a new challenge and both saw it at Leeds. Their approaches to it are perhaps not quite as different as they might appear.

The two men could not have been recruited in more different circumstances. Bielsa was wooed by Leeds director of football Victor Orta and chief executive Angus Kinnear, and they spoke football for hours, by which time Bielsa had already done his homework, watching every single Leeds game from the previous season, including friendlies. He showed minimal interest in talking money (he is reputedly the highest paid Leeds manager ever but pays his coaching staff from his own salary and recently donated £2m for a training ground at old club Newell's.)

By contrast, Leeds managing director Bill Fotherby courted Wilko in a motorway car park after the police helped him get his car out of the Elland Road car park to go and meet the prospective new boss. The club had lost three games in a row under Peter Gunby and fans were rioting. Fotherby took the contract to Wilkinson, scribbled the salary in Biro and Wilko signed it right there in that car park. Something about Leeds – thousands of miles from his own birthplace – touched Bielsa and intrigued him. It was a sleeping giant, a one club city with huge potential. Similar thoughts had passed through Wilko's mind some 30 years before. The Yorkshireman had and recognised that Wednesday – like every club – had a "ceiling", and that Leeds United's was potentially much higher. Like Bielsa, once he heard about the project, he didn't need too much persuading to sign on the dotted line.

Both men inherited a club, which had spent years in the doldrums. Leeds had languished in the second (and for one season) third tier for 15 years when Bielsa arrived, no less than 20 managers having failed to get them up. For Wilko, in 1988, it was six years since they'd been relegated under Allan Clarke and two other Leeds legends in Eddie Gray and Billy Bremner or Gunby had been able to reverse United's dismal fortunes. "It had become a sort of beaten up picture of the Revie days with this frame around it of bad behaviour," Wilkinson told me in 2011. "The club didn't own the ground and were in debt. The training ground was shit and we were bottom of the league." Not dissimilar to the state of the club at Bielsa's arrival – the bad behaviour was mostly long gone, but the other parallels were not dissimilar. Wilko also inherited a club run by a large, unwieldy board dominated by the city council, who owned the ground. At his insistence, a smaller power structure was established in which all major decisions were made by chairman Leslie Silver, Fotherby and director Peter Gilman, in conjunction with the new manager. Similarly, the tight power structure at Leeds now constitutes Kinnear, Orta and owner Andrea Radrizzani in close consultation with Bielsa. Significantly, one of Radrizzani's first actions on buying the club in 2017 was to buy back the ground.

Bielsa instigated a wind of change. The swimming pool at the Thorp Arch training ground was filled again for the first time in years. He changed the culture – a mark on a wall left by someone leaning a foot on it was seen as a mark of disrespect which would no longer be allowed to happen. Instead, he had his players picking up litter so they'd appreciate the struggles fans go through to earn money for tickets. Years before, Wilko's first action was to have the old "glory days" photos taken down because he felt people had been clinging to them. Norman "Bites Yer Legs" Hunter was removed from the coaching staff and Wilkinson redesigned the club badge. He wanted improvements to the stadium and set up the youth academy which to this day provides a production line of glittering young talent. He conceived Thorp Arch, which relocated training from the old Fullerton Park the bit of land opposite the stadium to the top-notch facility it still is today. Granted, it has now been reimagined to Bielsa's specifications, with beds and a relaxation area. With trademark attention to detail, the South American even complained that the light switches between the beds were off centre, and must be realigned.

Wilko made some shrewd marquee signings – one thinks of Lee Chapman or Gordon Strachan (a bargain discard from Manchester United he compared to "finding a Rolls Royce in a barn") in the second tier, then Gary McAllister and Tony Dorigo

MARCHANDO JUNTOS
DOS MIL VEINTE

2019
2020

after promotion. He also transformed underachieving or journeymen players into world beaters. Carl Shutt had been at non-league Spalding United before following Wilko from Wednesday along with league title-winning Mel Sterland, among others. Full back Micky Whitlow was picked up from non-league Witton Albion but now has a league title winners' medal. David Batty and Gary Speed came from the youth team, as does Kalvin Phillips, now one of the first names on Bielsa's team sheet and picking up caps for England.

Bielsa's reign started with a £7m outlay on striker Patrick Bamford (financed by selling young Ronaldo Vieira to Sampdoria) and Wolves left-back Barry Douglas but the bulk of his promotion squad was made up of loans (such as Spanish goalkeeper Kiko Casilla from Real Madrid or Jack Harrison from Manchester City) or players who'd not pulled up trees under previous managers. Liam Cooper, a 2014 recruit from Chesterfield, was dubbed "League One Liam" before Bielsa transformed him into a promotion-winning captain. At time of writing, the centre half doesn't look out of place in the Premier League. The same could be said of the ever-improving Luke Ayling, a 2016 arrival from Bristol City who'd previously spent four years at non-league Yeovil. Before Bielsa, Stuart Dallas had been in and out of the team in various positions for four years until he made the left back position his. Both managers (or coaches, to use a title the Argentine prefers) seem to have the knack of identifying hidden talents and polishing rough diamonds. Wilko mostly played the old 4-4-2. Bielsa employs a 4-1-4-1 or 3-3-1-3 (a system used at Newell's 30 years ago) if the opposition play two strikers. Sometimes, as recently against Wolves, his players change formations during a game, wingers often switch wings regularly and the "full backs" often look more like wingers too.

Bielsa's teams play beautiful, intricate but fiercely attacking football. He has been called "high priest of the high press", and possession can be as much as 70%. Wilko's teams were more direct, with Chapman very much the old-style centre forward, but similarly liked to play their football in the opposition half. On a good day – and there were many in 1991/92 – centre backs Chris Whyte and Chris Fairclough would marshall the half way line while their teammates steamrollered their opponents.

For both managers, trust is underpinned by science. Bielsa's players believe in his methods – even the notorious training game "murderball", eleven vs eleven with no stoppages or free-kicks and constant play – because they know they work. They obey commands to lose body fat and endure similar arduous pre-seasons as players did under Wilko, an avid nutritionist who sent his players on feared cross country runs.

Bielsa's minute analysis of opponents echoes Revie's infamous dossiers but monitoring his own players was something Wilkinson also did. Long before the onset of technology, "the Sarge" measured his players' performances using KPI's (key performance indicators) worked out with tape measures and a stopwatch. Bielsa puts much focus on repetition of certain drills, and his players seem to almost telepathically know where each other are. Wilko spent hours on set pieces on the grounds that they lead to goals.

Neither manager put much store by grand Churchillian team talks. However, each recognises the value of the right words at the right time. In his promotion season away at Sunderland's unforgiving Roker Park, Wilkinson prepared his players by telling them "We're going into the lions den and we're going to remove its teeth." In 1992 he used golfing metaphors and comradeship: "Trust your swing. Trust your fellow players". In Bielsa's promotion season – having fallen short in the final weeks at the first attempt the year before – he reportedly responded to a morale-shattering loss against Nottingham Forest by abandoning his usual video analysis and delivering a rousing speech that drew a round of applause.

When he was Leeds manager, Wilkinson lived on the outskirts of Sheffield in a new-build he lives in to this day. Bielsa rarely returns to Argentina and lives in a humble rented flat above a sweet shop in Wetherby, near Thorp Arch, from where he walks to work each day. Wilkinson was rarely seen by Leeds fans between matches. The permanently tracksuited Bielsa is often encountered shuffling into the local Morrisons or Costa. Two very different characters, two very different styles, but their spirit and their goals are indeed United.

Wilkinson won the league with a squad assembled for £8.1m, half the cost of runner-up Manchester United's. He told me that this feat was achieved because those players "performed to the very maximum of their limits for all those games". Shortly after returning to the top flight, Bielsa's Leeds went up against Guardiola's Manchester City – the 2018 and 2019 Premiership champions and the first billion pound squad in football history – and were unlucky to only draw. The Argentines verdict "We had to play to the limit" felt eerily similar to Wilko's words about 1992. The Yorkshireman took the club to English football's absolute summit. Whether that can ever be achieved by Bielsa or indeed any other Leeds manager is something only time will tell, but if both men have taught us anything it's that the seemingly impossible can be made possible. We can all dare to dream.

Dave Simpson —
Author of *The Last Champions – The Year That Football Changed Forever*, about the 1991/92 title season and onset of the Premiership.

UNI
WE
S

"You have to give great credit to Angus Kinnear and Andrea Radridziani for having the balls to approach him and then to get him to a second tier side in England. It's all about Marcelo Bielsa, a man of enormous presence and integrity who has made us all, fans, players, staff, better and more 'United' than I can remember.

Bielsa Ball baby!"

Ralph Ineson

MARCHING ON
TOGETHER
11
4
10
7

M
O
T

SUPER LEEDS
LEEDS

7

"We have to love our past, we need to remember we are a glorious club but now, the focus is not the past. It's the future!"

Andrea Radrizzani

"GO ON GARY SPEED,
GET ONE YOURSELF, SON!"
1969-2011

"BILLY PLAYED MORE WITH HIS HEART THAN HIS HEAD. HE HAD A HEART THE SIZE OF ELLAND ROAD."

EDDIE GRAY

4

IN MEMORY OF
OLIVER GORMAN
15.11.94 - 30.06.18
LUFC
MARK NICHOLLS
NOAH NICHOLLS
FATHER & SON
JAMIE KERSHAW
STUART KERSHAW
DAVE CARTHY
TRAMORE '78
LUFC
LEO GOTTLIFFE
ALWAYS IN OUR
HEARTS
SCOTT & ADAM
HORNER - LUFC
MANJIT HAYRE
BFD WHITES
LUFC
ANDREW DEVANEY
ELLIOT DEVANEY
KOP SINCE 1988
LUFC
BOB CROSSLEY
1946 - 2018
FOREVER LEEDS
LUFC
CHRIS CURDY
1959 - 2018
FOREVER LEEDS
PHILIP DARLEY
LUFC FOREVER
BRIAN FISHER
16.08.1940
LUFC
TREVOR HORSLEY
HAPPY BIRTHDAY
CARL & MATTY
DAN WALKER '88
FOREVER LUFC
HELGE BERG
LUFC NORWAY
LUFC
TREV TOM BEN
THE GILLAM'S
LEYBURN
JOSEPH CRISP
18TH BIRTHDAY
CLARK & NOLAN
FAMILY LUFC
LUFC
CHRISTINE
WHARTON
MOT
WESLEY LOMAX
FOREVER LEEDS
WALKER FAMILY
MIRFIELD
LUFC
GORDON, KATIE
ALICE & ETHAN
FRIEL - MOT
LUFC
TONY HICKEY
1959-2018
LEEDS WARRIOR
LUFC
ASHLEY WOOD
18-03-1991
NIGEL SEAL
FOREVER LOVED
LUFC
NOEL & FRAN
PHELAN IRELAND
HONEYMOON 1974
JACK CAULFIELD
MOT
DAD - ROCHEY
FOREVER LEEDS
LUFC
CHRIS STARR
JACOB STARR
HOME & AWAY
JUD & ROSE
DANNY & KOBY
LUFC
LUFC
WILLIAM MARTIN
MOT SINCE 1957
LEEDS FOREVER
SUE DAVIES
WE LOVED MUM
GARETH CONNER
LOVE MUM LUFC
LUFC
MARK B SMITH
ALWAYS LOVED
DAD AND JAMES
LUFC
IN MEMORY OF
CHRIS DENSHAW
1957-2014
LUFC
DAD & DAVID
LUFC FOREVER
MOT

JACK
CHARLTON
MANDY HUNTER
ONE TRUE LOVE
WE ARE LEEDS X
MARCHING ON TOGETHER
DANISH SUPPORTERS
OF LEEDS UNITED
ANDREW TEALE
FOREVER LEEDS
BUSK FAMILY DK
LEEDS FOREVER
ALEX PEEL
ROBERT PEEL
ALEC PEEL
GRANDAD & LEAH
BUTTERWORTH
DOREEN COOPER
MILLIE BURROWS
MICHAEL & CALLUM
SCOTT & NATHAN
SENIOR
GAZ ROBERTSON
HAPPY BIRTHDAY
WARREN WOOD
LEEDS FOREVER
ROBERT
FLETCHER
TOM BARRITT
LUFC FOREVER
MICK PARKER
FOREVER LEEDS
DANIEL SENIOR
LOVE YOU DADDY
FROM NOLA
RICHARD HOOLE
HARRY HOOLE
WE ARE LEEDS
DARREN DOYLE
CO FERMANAGH
BARRY HOPE 58
NICKY HOPE 89
DANNY CARR

YORKSHIRE
Evening Post

LEEDS UNITED
CHARLIE
LUFC

“My first ever Leeds game was with my brother, who has now sadly passed away. Leeds Vs Swindon in the League Cup. We are losing and in the 90th minute our goalkeeper Paul Robinson goes up for a corner. The ball comes in and he jumps, wins the header and scores... I knew right then that football was the sport for me! The buzz was unreal!”

Danny Cullen

OUR THING

Ruth Saxton

As a child, whenever we passed Elland Road on car journeys, it was a bit like who can see the sea first; waiting for the top of one of the beacon-like diamond floodlights to come into view. As you drove past, eyes glued to the window, you wouldn't look away, just in case you got to see something. Anything. Like Charlie Bucket at the gates of the chocolate factory. I now live five minutes' walk from the ground and see it every day. But even though it's so familiar, it has never lost that sense of magic.

I couldn't tell you when my love for Leeds United started. It was simply an expectation in our house; the norm. My dad was Leeds-born. As was his dad. And you supported Leeds.

It definitely helped the cause early on when Tommy Wright, Scott Sellars and Denis Irwin came to my primary school. As one of the two girls (yes, two) who liked football, I was reluctantly allowed to join in. The same year there was a school trip to Elland Road, where we had a long chat with manager, Eddie Gray, and it was firmly implanted in my heart.

It wasn't too long after that my dad eventually relented and I went to my first game. Don't ask me who it was against or what the score was (I know! I know!) but I could still describe the sounds, sights and smells like it was yesterday. It even appears in my mind's eye from the vantage of a small child. I think I was about ten. My brother used to go in the Boys' Pen before that but I was a girl, so I had to wait until I was considered old enough.

After a couple of years' nagging, and a promotion at work for dad, we got season tickets for 1989/90 and seats in the North West Corner's Family Stand: dad, brother and me. During half-time, a player used to come and sign your programme and you got cards at Christmas and your birthday. Like many people, I remember that season as being much less stressful than it was. I suspect my brain has subliminally cut the trauma out in order I continue to go back year in year out. I think my favourite game that season, and possibly ever at Elland Road, was the Sheffield United 'Go on Gary Speed, get one yourself son!' 4–0 trouncing. Again, it's so clear. The ground was rocking; we were all just laughing in disbelief. That euphoria we continually chase as fans. There's also the memory of sitting in the garden listening to the radio, waiting for confirmation of promotion; agony!

My brother only came for one season, so Leeds United was just dad and me; our thing.

Memories that stand out are mixed. There's the time we went to Oldham away and were kept in the ground after the game. We'd lost and people were fed up so started pelting the scoreboard with stones and smashing the lights. As they let us out, the crowd surged. I wasn't worried until I saw the fear on my dad's face as he struggled to keep me safe beneath his out-stretched arms.

A more light-hearted moment was walking down Beeston Hill on game day after a night out with my friends. I was about 15. My dad looked down at my trousers. "What's that poking out the bottom of your jeans?" Mortified, I hurriedly picked up last night's knickers. I don't think he'd stopped laughing, even by the time we got to the ground.

In the mid-90s I moved away to study and work. But we'd try catch a game whenever I came home. And of course we'd ring each other with any major news. In fact, I'd just started my first job in London in 1998 when he called the office... to play me live coverage of David Batty's press conference, when he re-signed for Leeds. My dad held the telephone to the telly and shouted a running commentary from the background, whilst I suppressed my excitement from my new boss, pretending I was on an important business call. A compilation video of the coverage landed in the post not long after.

When I moved back to Leeds in 2002, we naturally and immediately picked up where we left off. Not-so great timing. Relegation quickly followed. Sometimes on the cold wintry nights of League One it felt like we should be getting paid to go.

When I moved to Holbeck he was thrilled, he had a personal parking space! So he'd turn up and we'd wander over together, usually with him telling me about the team and the game we hadn't even watched yet. He was an expert, you know (typical teacher)!

And then we'd walk back. And I'd just want to digest it, or forget it. Or even, on those rare occasions when we'd won, just enjoy it. But he'd have to analyse it, sometimes giving me opinions I'd previously given him...but he'd never admit to that!

Three seasons ago he got cancer and stopped coming. So I'd go and watch televised away games with him on the sofa. One of the best was when Bielsaball was relatively new and we watched, gobsmacked, as Leeds made a mockery of Frank Lampard's Derby County. It was like Sheffield United 89/90 all over again. At one point, my dad stopped watching the screen as he was enjoying my delight more. And we were laughing together in disbelief once again.

I love Leeds United. It's unconditional. My dad taught me that much. But it's deeper than that, because Leeds United gave us a connection when we struggled to find one. I had been a total daddy's girl. Then puberty struck and he was shelved for music and boys. But luckily we had LUFC. So over the years, when he was wrong about everything, when he wasn't cool enough, when I was living in another country, when he didn't understand my jobs, when I didn't get married or have children, there was always Leeds United...

Last year my dad died. His last text message to me was something humdrum and 'everyday' but hugely important about Leeds United. And in his final days we shared long nights in St. Gemma's Hospice, when it felt like the rest of the world was asleep, singing Leeds songs together.

Right until the very end, it was our thing.

Ruth Saxton —
Contributes to *The Square Ball* and works as a Community Producer for *Slung Low*.

YH13 NHD
L44DS P
ERT

WINNEBAGO

Clipper

globalautocare.co.uk
Global
A WORLD OF AUTO CARE
LAND ROAD

"To be loved is this biggest title, bigger than the Champions League or the Premier League or whatever. To be loved is the most important thing and I think Marcelo has that more than any other manager in the world."

Pep Guardiola

"Elland Road is a very special place to me and thousands like me. I am of a generation that started out in the Scratching Shed, taken to the games by my family members. I then graduated to the Boy's Pen on Lowfields Road. Further rites of passage meant standing in the Kop, left or right side depending on which part of Leeds you came from. In my years I have seen the good, bad and the ugly at our home and 'place of worship.' The good, titles being won and great European football nights. The bad times relegation, tears and administration. The ugly, a succession of bad owners pillaging our club for all they could take and plenty more tears.

Now we can revel again in top flight football, with good owners and honest players. In these difficult times I can't wait to go back and enjoy Elland Road again."

Hayden Evans

adidas

48'

BAMFORD

62'

HERNÁNDEZ

66'

BAMFORD

"One I'll never forget was Millwall at home last season. Leeds losing 2–0 at half time but Elland Road was still bouncing. It was like the entire stadium knew we were still going to smash 'em and guess what... We did smash them, with the game ending 3–2!!!!! I shouted myself hoarse that game which is ridiculous behaviour for a 37 year old but that's what supporting Leeds United and a Tuesday night under the lights at Elland Road does to you."

Matt Bowman

Clipper
Logistics evolved
Clipper
www.clippergroup.co.uk
Clipper
wish
Clipper

TransUnion

DIRTY
DIRTY
DIRTY

LEEDS
LEEDS
LEEDS

MARCELO BIELSA BEATS AN UNSHAK-ABLE SENSE OF DOOM

Neil Jeffries

It gets overwhelming, sometimes. At other moments you may forget. But being a Leeds United fan is something that never really goes away. It's odd to think that we probably remember the bad bits as vividly as the good. Right now we can clearly remember where we were on that Friday night when Huddersfield Town – of all teams – beat the otherwise impressive West Bromwich Albion to guarantee our promotion back to the Premier League. I vividly recall being annoyed that Huddersfield had scored first to put us in that position. In text messages to friends I moaned that, in that most difficult of seasons, I wanted Leeds to continue to do it the hard way and clinch promotion with something we could claim as our own – a Patrick Bamford goal, say – on the final day of the season. I was appalled at the thought that we might feel beholden to anyone else. It was probably because over 50 years of being a Leeds fan had imbued me with an unshakable sense of doom. If something could go wrong, it probably would. After all, it had happened at the end of the season before. That's why until the referee blew his whistle on that Friday night I refused to let myself believe that in added-time West Brom wouldn't equalise to make it 2–2, or win, so that 16 years of mostly missed opportunities would stretch to 17, then 18, and more. Had someone told me we would win the Championship by a stunning 10-point margin I wouldn't have believed them. Had they then argued that time travel had been invented and Leeds had really done this, I'd have found the confirmation of time travel easier to accept. But, hey, we *did* win by 10 points and we *are* embarking on a Premier League campaign with Marcelo Bielsa as head coach. Something else about as likely as proof of time travel back in May 2018 when Paul Heckingbottom's 16th game in charge saw us end the Championship season in 13th place with Dutchman Ouasim Bouy still considered a defensive option on the bench. It had, though, been so much worse.

Although the calamitous financial planning of a former chairman whose name I still can't utter without spitting in disgust saw Leeds bereft, bankrupt and belittled come 2004, I think that for me the utter nadir came on Sunday 30th November 2008 at the Glass World Stadium in Histon, Cambridgeshire. In a heavy and constant downpour, a miserable and inconsistent Leeds were knocked out of the FA Cup – at Second Round stage, note – by non-league Histon United. True, we were playing in the third tier of English football at that stage and Eastern Counties League side Histon were only two divisions below us in the pyramid, but that really HURT. Making matters just that little bit worse, the whole sorry 90-minute nightmare were broadcast live to the nation by BBC's Match Of The Day cameras so no one could be in any doubt about how far we had fallen. It added further humiliation that, coached by our magnificent former player Gary McAllister, a near full-strength side had tried but simply failed to outclass their part-time opponents. I later learned that several of the cameras, planted on temporary scaffold platforms, were broadcasting through lenses plagued by condensation or raindrops. I also discovered that it was the only game played in the county that day as the weather had seen all others rained off. But misty images and a pudding of a pitch couldn't spare our blushes or excuse our embarrassment as the game was settled by a goal scored by a postman. Leeds were down *and* out.

We've since exited the FA Cup at the hands of Newport County and Sutton United but, being old enough to remember the humiliation of losing 3–2 at Colchester in February 1971, I was prepared for that. (And this time I wouldn't be taunted by all and sundry about the result the following Monday at school.) I was at Wembley when Second Division Sunderland beat us in the 1973 FA Cup final. (Followed by another terrible day at school.) But Histon was the worst. Everything else, particularly all those runners-up slots under Don Revie, were at least preceded by a tidal wave of excellence and could always be blamed in part on bad luck. Not Histon. That was the bottom of the barrel.

The memory of which makes how things have turned around under Marcelo Bielsa all the more dizzying. I'm not certain that director of football Victor Orta and chairman Andrea Radrizzani fully understood what they were taking on when they flew to Argentina to meet Bielsa in a Buenos Aires hotel in an attempt to persuade one of the planet's greatest football coaches to take on Leeds United. It was a mission that even the eternal optimist Orta had described as "impossible". In fact – given the language barrier, Bielsa's age (he was 63 when they met and perfectly entitled to be considering retirement), and Leeds' own predicament as a hopelessly average second-tier mid-table side – it might more accurately have been described as "insane". Hadn't Bielsa left his previous job at Lille in 2017 after less than half a season – suspended by his own club with just 13 games played? And hadn't he quit his previous appointment – at Lazio in July 2016 – after just two days due to disagreements with the club's owners? Well, yes. And yet... There was clearly something about Leeds – the city, its people and the history of the club – that touched Bielsa's heart. "I was convinced by the strength of Leeds as a club and as an institution," he later said. When Orta and Radrizzani first met him, Bielsa had already sourced and watched videos of Leeds and all their Championship opponents – and could quote statistics on the success of various formations used by each. He knew Leeds and the division they'd be playing in as well as any man in England. Better, as it turned out. Incredibly, he'd even acquired architects drawings of the Thorp Arch training facilities and indicated how he wanted the building changed.

They flew home shell-shocked, impressed and tormented by the fact that they had talked about everything except a contract. But one was signed on 15th June 2018 and after that everything about Leeds United changed.

Others, such as Luke Ayling have reported how they proudly stepped onto scales believing they were at the peak of physical condition, only to be told they were a kilo and a half overweight. So they went away, improved their diet – and returned even fitter. Even now, each member of the squad is weighed every day. In the background Bielsa and his team were undertaking the kind of in-depth analysis of opposition performances and statistics that would have made the work done by Maurice Lindley, Les Cocker et al for Don Revie's famous dossiers seem like a brief glance at the back of the Daily Mirror.

Most importantly there were the training sessions. The sort of stuff mere mortals like football fans couldn't begin to understand

but can certainly appreciate. When a few details leaked out they made perfect sense... How come *all* teams didn't make their training pitches the same as the one in their own stadium?
Why shouldn't you be as adept as controlling a lobbed pass *while standing on an unsteady air-filled dome* as you would with your foot planted firmly on grass? And, if a game lasts 90 minutes but includes a lot of interruptions for re-starts, wouldn't you clearly be among the fittest in your division if in training you regularly play for 90 minutes *non-stop*, not pausing even for a throw-in because someone had rolled another ball into play? At first they called it 'Bielsaball', these days 'Murderball'. Hard work. There's no substitute for it in any walk of life.

And so with only a few new additions, the team that had so disappointed us in 2017/18 looked almost unbeatable in Bielsa's first season. Amazon Prime brought in cameras, got unbelievable access, hired Russell Crowe to narrate... and almost made the most feel good documentary of all time with Take Us Home. Except that, this being Leeds United, it all went horribly wrong at the end. Which meant Leeds United had to try again in 2019/20.

This time not even a global pandemic and a 354-day season completed behind closed doors could put a spanner in the works and Leeds played beautiful football all over again – with no sense of panic, fatigue or fear of ultimate failure – to top the final table by those 10 beautiful points. Extraordinary.

Perhaps the most extraordinary thing about what Bielsa has done to the team is how well they continue to perform in the level above. They forced champions Liverpool to concede three goals before stealing the narrowest of victories at Anfield... They did not buckle even as Manchester City pushed them "to the limit" (Bielsa's words) at Elland Road but instead held on for a draw.

Much has been made of the mutual respect between Bielsa and City's Pep Guardiola. Guardiola is the man who Barcelona, Bayern Munich and most recently City – one of the planet's richest clubs – rated as the best coach in the world. Apart from a few vocal ticks, his and Bielsa's quotes about each other are interchangeable. Each speaks of the other's unique style, the entertainment it provides, and how it is impossible to imitate.

"Bielsa," says Guardiola, "is probably the person I have admired the most in world football. As a manager and as a person... He's unique. His teams are always a joy to watch, how honest they are. They want to attack. They want to produce some good football for spectators." High praise indeed. And in his remark about creating "good football" for the spectators – you and I – lays the absolute crux of Bielsa. For him, the beautiful game is *all* about style. Better players can improve it, increase its efficiency (to use another Bielsa term) but attempt at that style guides everything Leeds United now do.

As he said at the end of Take Us Home: "I came to be part of a programme that has goals, and of course we are aware of the goals wanted by the city and the club, the players, the fans, everybody. But I also can't say that my only interest is winning. What also interests me is the way we build to the victory." Bielsa sets our team targets that are not measured in points or league positions. Those targets are working hard to produce an entertaining style that

Neil Jeffries —
Editor of *Leeds Leeds Leeds* magazine for 13 years and also works on all things loud, with *Classic Rock Magazine* and all things Leeds, on the matchday programme.

– if all else is equal – will deliver goals, points and improved league positions. Not long after promotion was secured, proud chairman Radrizzani described Bielsa as "the perfect fit" for Leeds United, and reviewed the statistics: "Possession, chances created, style of play – his team is top in everything."

Whatever else happens, I'll settle for being overwhelmed by that alone. And take pride in that.

Thank you, Marcelo.

BURTON

Maintain social distancing. Keep two metres apart.
32Red

Leeds City Museum
FREE ENTRY
FAST X SLOW
FASHION

"The supporters, the only thing for them is that they love their club. The only thing they receive in exchange is emotions. For this reason the supporter is the best thing in football. This is going to be a lovely memory for all my life and it was beautiful. Everything that happened was so, so beautiful.

Unforgettable!"

Marcelo Bielsa

ENTERPRISE

THE LEEDS INSTITUTE
LEEDS CITY MUSEUM
AREN'T WE
32Red

PREMIER 2021

"Bielsa gave us hope, and the belief that there was light at the end of a 16-year tunnel. I wanted to paint the end of the tunnel!"

Andy McVeigh (Burley Banksy)

BIELSA STAYS
VAMOS
LEEDS
CARAJO

MARCELO
@pantsdanny
Burley BanKsy
IN
BIELSA
WE
TRUST

VIEW FROM THE HILL

James Brown

I like looking at Elland Road. From the hill, from the train, from the street. I first went there as a very young boy in the early 70s for a night game with my granddad. I've no memory of who we were playing, just that we were sitting high up in the West Stand. The pitch seemed miles away. The players were booting out plastic balls with their faces and autographs printed on them, so it must have been the Paul Trevillion period, maybe the 1971/72 season. That's my first memory, the green pitch at night. I started going regularly in about 1975 or 76. A couple of friends and I would take the number 1 or the 4 bus all the way from The Original Oak in Headingley, past where I got off for school in Woodhouse, through the city centre, past the start of the motorway and out and up the hill to Beeston. Then we would walk down the short terraced roads and look down the hill at the ground. That's the way I mostly arrive now, decades later. I sometimes take a taxi from the station but if I drive from somewhere in Leeds with mates, or all the way from London where I live, we park in that same area and walk to the edge of that hill where I stop and look down at the ground. Taking in the sight, letting the expectation wash through me. Believing something good will happen, knowing it might not. A 400-mile round-trip is a lot further for a 0–0 draw with Bolton than a 1–1 draw with Barcelona.

Standing there, my eye is naturally drawn to the small pitch to the right halfway down the hill. The one they used as a training ground in The Damned United film. I like the fact that there's an amateur pitch just up from Elland Road. It's a reminder that it's all the same game. There's no one who has played on that amateur pitch who hasn't dreamt of playing at Elland Road.

The home of LUFC is not a great looking ground. When I glimpse it from a train, as passengers start getting ready to disembark, or look up at it surrounded by the matchday crowds, I never admired its architectural presence. It's just a place with the most intense collection of emotions I've experienced. That's what I feel when I see it up close, from Beeston Hill, or flashing past on train tracks. A connection.

I like the collections of players, the number 7s and so on, that they've added to the exterior of the East Stand now. They provide visual references to those emotions and memories. During really intense games I lose myself. I struggle to recapture results and line-ups but remember moments and feelings.

For a while in the late 90s and early 2000s I worked with the club producing the official magazine, *Leeds Leeds Leeds*, which Justin shot most of the covers for. It meant I had tickets in the Director's Box and access to the fine dining experience in the corporate hospitality area. It meant I could turn to Bobby Charlton after we'd hammered Fergie's Man U and tell him he needed to get a new manager. It meant a mate could come after me and say, "What did you say to Bobby Charlton? He was furious!"

It was a very different experience to when I went in the Kop with my mates as a kid. The head of operations, a man called David Spencer, did a fantastic job with the food. It was as good as any high end restaurant. The place was always buzzing with excitement. Guests, wearing ill-fitting suits and awkward ties on a company day out. The bar staff and behind-the-scenes ladies at Leeds, who ran the place, were as swept up in the atmosphere of matchday as the fans and the players.

I liked being the first into to or last out of the dining room because I'd encounter the stragglers, the people who had spent so much time on the pitch and pitch-side themselves they knew what was coming and didn't feel compelled to rush out.

The week we were courting Leicester City's Martin O'Neill to replace George Graham, I met the legendary Crystal Palace and Man City coach Malcolm Allison at the bar. We were the only people in the huge Banqueting Suite. I bought him a brandy and he thanked me and called me "a scholar", a very 70s drinking term. He told me he thought Martin, as he called him, would be a great manager for Leeds. I loved that moment.

Most weeks I would see John Charles in there, we'd be among the last in the toilets before making our way to the pitch.

I used to think about everything he'd experienced at Leeds and in Italy and how much of it remained unsaid and untold in his head. It's not the sort of opening line you can come up with when you are standing next to a man in the bogs.

After the matches I would wait until the crowds and traffic jams had cleared before I'd attempt to head off.

On a small, easily assembled stage, Keith Parkinson would bring out Lee Bowyer and a local businessman would present him with a Man of the Match award. After this as the tables were emptying and the catering staff took plates of half-eaten sandwiches and cakes back into the kitchens, I would walk past the weird collection of gifts and trophies in the cabinets in the corporate area and back up the steps to the stand.

I'd look out over the empty stands and down onto the bright green pitch I'd first seen decades before where a trainer would be warming down unused subs and a groundsman would be prodding turf with a fork.

I'd hear the clatter of seats as security staff and litter pickers checked the rows. And I'd think... this is mine. Just as everyone else does. Leeds United is ours. And that's why I like looking at Elland Road.

James Brown —
Author of *Above Head Height* and creator of
Leeds Leeds Leeds and *Loaded* magazines.

"Leeds United is a very special club to me in many ways. It is where I enjoyed my life and my career, with loads of moments, friendships and experiences that made me. To have spent more than ten years of my life at the club and then be rewarded with a testimonial was an amazing honour. Seeing everyone appreciate my contribution to the team was really special and full of emotions for me. Especially having my family and parents there at the ground."

Lucas Radebe

Akse P19 — *Paving the Way*

32Red
WELCOME TO
ELLAND ROAD
#TheOnlyPlaceForUs
PROGRAMMES

32Red
THE FOURS
FANTASTIC FOURS
THE FIVES
FAMOUS FIVES
THE SEVENS
MAGNIFICENT SEVENS
THE NINES
SUBLIME NINE
32Red

BURGERS
CHEESEBURGERS
HOT DOGS
CHEESE DOGS
CHIP BUTTIES
CHIPS
CHIPS & CURRY
Why not try our
1/2lb
Bacon
Double
Cheeseburger
Kappa
LEEDS

VERY
THE OLD PEACOCK

"Well you know it's as if I was one of them. I felt every up and down and pain and joy like a family member. You obviously don't know every fan but when you meet one, it's as if you click and have something in common straight away."

Andrew Hughes

ENTRANCE
6
SENIOR
WARNING

LEEDS
LEEDS
LEEDS

"I have many match day memories, one in particular was when I used to shoot pictures on the halfway line. Between the dugouts there was a TV camera position and I was allowed to use it when there was no TV coverage. One game when Howard Wilkinson was manager he kept getting in my way. It was quite an aggressive game, so I jokingly mentioned this to the Commercial manager at the time Bob Baldwin that he should have a word and tell him to stay in his seat, thinking he knew it was a joke. Unfortunately, for me he didn't and he told Wilkinson word for word, who responded with 'OK I'll stay at home and we'll just play the game for the photographers then.'

At least Wilko saw the funny side, he greeted me with a grin the next time he saw me."

Andrew Varley
45th Season as Leeds United Club Photographer

LEEDS UNITED
Welcomes You
NORTH
WEST
EAST
SOUTH
LOWFIELDS ROAD

WELCOME TO
ELLAND ROAD
ENTERPRISE

Global
ELLAND ROAD

SOCK TAGS, SKOL & JIMMY ARMFIELD'S PIPE

Craig Ferguson

Why do you do it to yourself?... Why do you put yourself through it?

Amazingly, no-one has ever actually said that to me. Except me, myself. That little voice in my head.

You know the feeling. Leeds lose a match, and that result completely ruins the rest of my day, the whole weekend, sometimes the whole week. I avoid anything that might remind me of the disappointment – papers, TV coverage, websites, people.
This has been uncomfortably frequent in recent years.
Well, the best part of 20 years, actually.

So why DO I do it?...

It's springtime, 1968... My older brothers, Pete and Ian, are busy adding new cuttings from the *Evening Post*, the 'Green Final' – remember that? – and the *Sunday Express* to their scrapbooks. I ask them what they're doing and why. 'We won a cup, the League Cup', comes the reply. *We?* We won a cup? There was never any question of me not being a Leeds fan. We're in Normanton, West Yorkshire, 20 minutes on the train from Leeds. Of course I'm a Leeds fan. I'm instantly hooked...

A year later, we're League Champions for the first time – I know because I had the two-page colour photo of the team with the trophy, pulled out of *Goal* magazine, stuck in pride of place on the wall behind my bed. And there alongside, in a photo on his own, is Mick Jones. He's my hero. There's a whole team of heroes, some more celebrated than others, but he's mine, our Number 9, centre-forward, top scorer in our first title-winning season. Our Ian will get me a pair of Number 9 sock-tags like Mick Jones' a couple of years later. I wear them even when I haven't got my Leeds kit on.

Christmas that same year, I get my first full footy kit – a major milestone in any football-mad kid's life. But mine's the best, it's a Leeds kit. Absolutely all-white, no trim, no sponsor back then, with a heavy cotton shirt with the classic owl badge carefully sewn on. Add that to getting Subbuteo table football too...
best Christmas ever.

It's November 1970 and I can hardly hide my excitement as me and Ian step off the bus into the thousands milling around Elland Road. It's my first match and it feels as brilliant as I dreamt it would. I climb the steps up into the old Lowfields Road Stand and stop still, looking out onto the magnificence of the pitch, hardly able to breath. I'm not big enough to see everything from the terraces but I see enough – my heroes in the flesh, in their pomp. Leeds 3 Blackpool 1. Future manager, Jimmy Armfield is playing left back for the visitors. smoking a pipe... but I couldn't swear to that. It might have taken a bus and a train to get us back to Normanton but I felt like I was floating home.

FA Cup Final Day 1972, and the whole family sits down to watch the full build-up, the match and the aftermath, as we always do. Two years earlier, we'd done the full package with Leeds scarves and rosettes festooned around the living room – especially on the telly – only for the Mighty Whites to fall to the Dirty Blues of

Chelsea after a replay. 1972 is different; we were sure it would be, and it is. *Jones... Clarke... one-nil.* We relive Sniffer's winner many times in my last few weeks in primary school, replete with David Colemanesque commentary.

Two years on, we're League Champions again and acknowledged by all as worthy Champions. On an early summer evening, Billy Bremner holds the trophy aloft before, and after his post-season Testimonial match at Elland Road. The game itself – a 0–0 draw against Sunderland – is a non-event, not the revenge we hoped for. But no-one cares. It looks and feels like a golden moment. We're celebrating being Top Dogs again, and we're going to be there or there abouts for a long time. *Aren't we?*

It's 1990 and we've spent years in the football wilderness. Eight years out of the top-flight feels twice as long. Unbearable. But we started to believe better times could lie ahead when the Chairman aimed for the stars and managed to persuade highly respected coach from exotic South Yorkshire to take up the reins. Howard Wilkinson – some of us had even heard of him. But would he take a chance on us? He does and at the end of his second season, he delivers. It takes a narrow victory over Bournemouth on a sunny Bank Holiday to clinch promotion. I listen on the radio in an empty house and celebrate with a can of *Skol*. We start a new decade with faith restored. Sound familiar?

In 1992, we're the Last Champions to win the old-school title. We're in 'pinch me, tell me I'm not dreaming' territory. Like all Leeds fans, I enjoy the best Sunday ever. What usually feels like the last solemn march to the start of another week in work or school, is the most joyous of Sundays – a 3–2 win at Brammall Lane followed by a Liverpool win over Manchester United and the surreal sight of four of our team (funny French fella included) sat on a sofa, all just as amazed by events as us, the fans. Living in Manchester at the time, the evening's festivities are particularly sweet with all my City-supporting pals buying me drinks, and even those from the dark side coming out to congratulate me (for getting very drunk and smiling like an ecstatic idiot).

I start writing for the club's official magazine in 1997, going on to meet and interview some of my all-time heroes... a full team and more. David Harvey, Trevor Cherry, Jack Charlton, Chrissie Fairclough, Tony Dorigo, Gordon Strachan, Tony Currie, Gary Speed, Eddie Gray, Joe Jordan, and yes, Mick Jones. I get to sit in Mick Jones's front room and ask him about some of the great games that I, as a boy, saw him play in, on the telly in my Mam and Dad's front room. I drive away from his house thinking it will probably never get better than that.

In the middle of the dark agonies of 'The Second Wilderness', there's cause for celebration in 2010. We have the glory of beating the old enemy in the Cup at the Theatre of Mediocrity but in true Leeds style, it somehow threatens to derail our Promotion train, as we lose focus on the last stretch of the journey. Sat with the boys from *Leeds Leeds Leeds* watching that tortuous, decisive match against Bristol Rovers, we feel like we've won the Champions League rather than a place in the Championship. It feels good that we can congratulate Simon Grayson in the press conference afterwards when most of the crabby old journos around us are

clearly begrudging us this taste of success.

And finally, it's 2020. 16 years out of the top-flight feels twice as long. Unbearable. But we started to believe better times could lie ahead when the Chairman aimed for the stars and managed to persuade highly-respected coach from exotic Argentina to take up the reins.

Marcelo Bielsa – most of us had never even heard of him. But would he take a chance on us? He does and at the end of his second season, he delivers. In the middle of a pandemic, we sit in Bucko's man-den watching on his new 50-inch screen. We need to celebrate together – we deserve to celebrate together. Two of my kids, Ruby and Billy, join in the champagne toast as we rub Derby's noses in our glory. A champagne celebration of champagne football. Days later, we celebrate again as we lift that same trophy that we'd first lifted in 1969.

And so, 50 years on from my first taste of football at Elland Road, it somehow feels like the circle is complete. Back now where I was then, tasting the good times, waiting for more. That's why I do it; that's why we do it. We can stomach eight years littered with spoilt weekends and bouts of disappointment that hurt like a kick in the nuts, 16 years even, if we know we'll have our day again – loving the rise from being written off and seeing the raising of silverware. We keep the faith.

Yep. That's why we do it.

Craig Ferguson —
Craig Ferguson wrote regularly for *Leeds Leeds Leeds* magazine between 1997 and 2012 whilst working as a TV screenwriter.

"Elland Road can either motivate or scare you to death. I loved walking down the tunnel to 'Marching on Together', that inspired me so much. I do know of many opposition players who have folded even before a ball had been kicked. Elland Road is an iconic football stadium with fantastic memories for me and for so many great players of LUFC.

Many times the crowd would suck the ball into the goal late on in games when I was manager to win a game."

Simon Grayson

lobal
A WORLD OF AUTO CARE
Our garage services are now open to all fans
Global
www.globalautocare.co.uk
Telephone: 0113 391 8045
HOME OF LEEDS UNITED
ELLAND ROAD

EXIT
KEEP CLEAR
S 1A
EXIT
KEEP CLEAR

"It's weird when you reflect back on the past being a Leeds United fan. My first season was the 00/01 and I went to the games with my old man. We had a good team, flying high in the league and in Europe. However, it was not until we were relegated that my love grew stronger for the club. Why? I think it's a mixture of 'everyone hates us,' so we had to stand tall together. Showing loyalty through the hard times and the desire to stick two fingers up to everyone when we return.

Obviously, for me the world title fight will always be a very special memory in my Elland Road experiences, but a stand out moment personally will always be the Bristol Rovers game in 2010. We had a good season that year. Some good cup wins and great crowd attendances. That Bristol game had everything and it was all riding on that day. Played in front of the biggest crowd of the season, it started badly. One of our standout players that year Max Gradel got sent off. Next we go a goal down. Losing 1–0 at half time and everyone in the ground is nervous but at the same time still believing and the hope is still alive. The local boy, Howson comes on as sub and scores a 20-yard equaliser. Then man of the moment Beckford pounces six yards out and scores the winner! The ground erupts! Pitch invasion and a Promotion!

I was sat in the North East Corner that game and when I got home, my ears were ringing for hours afterwards. I felt numb and tingly all at the same time, a lovely feeling that I didn't want to end."

Josh Warrington

Global
A WORLD OF AUTO
HOME OF LEEDS UNITED
ELLAND ROAD

MATCHDAY TICKET COLLECTIONS ONLY
IN
Buses from here

ELLAND ROAD
HOME OF

"IT WOULD BE A DREAM FOR ME, TO SEE LEEDS UNITED BACK IN THE PREMIER LEAGUE IN MY LIFETIME."

NORMAN HUNTER

WELCOME TO
ELLAND ROAD
#TheOnlyPlaceForUs
BITE
YER
LEGS
NORMAN
Packard Bell
NORMAN
BITES
your Legs
RIP

REST IN PEACE
TREVOR

ONE CHURCH,
ELLAND ROAD,
ONE GOD, DON REVIE
KEEP THE FAITH
THANK YOU FOR
GETTING ME TO
WEMBLEY
PAUL TREVILLION

13
Billy Bremner - Leeds United
Prints £5 each
SPECIAL OFFER
5 prints
for £20
VISA
PRINT 3
SPECIAL OFFER
LEEDS UNITED A.F.C.
Leeds United - First Division Champions
1968 -1969
SPECIAL OFFER
PRINTS £5 EACH
OR

"People often ask me if I support Leeds? I tell them no I support Wrexham, where I grew up, but when Pablo scored at Swansea, I shrieked. When Huddersfield scored against West Brom, I ran up and down the room crazily hugging people. After nearly 30 years living in Leeds, I think I've got it. It's a very special football club."

Bryn Law

Logistics evolved
www.clippergroup.co.uk
32Red

OFFICIAL
MERCHANDISE
32Red
Kappa
32Red

HOW MUCH DO YOU THINK YOU'VE SPENT SUPPORTING LEEDS?

Chris Madden

'How much do you think you've spent supporting Leeds?'

Ever been asked that question? You've possibly started totting it up in your head a few times.

Season/match ticket, away days, bus/coach/train/petrol, fish butty/cheesy chips in the caff, programme, Square Ball, couple of pints in ER, replica shirt (home & away), those trips to Europe if you were lucky enough (flights + hotel + sustenance). Then the kids came along so chuck in the nippers' ticket, matchday trawl around the club shop, bottle of pop, crisps, sweets TIMES BY how many seasons is it now?

Of course you haven't done the maths, only an idiot would do that, because there isn't a price is there? I mean, we all know there is but it's not monetary, it goes way beyond that. You and I well know the emotional cost don't we? Sixteen plus years have served us a stark diet of mostly cold barely edible scraps punctuated by the occasional promise of an Emperor's feast.

And yet, if you don't get it you just don't get it. Across those years you've probably been taunted with the old '22 grown men kicking a pig's bladder around a field' quip a fair bit. You have to forgive them because if you don't follow football it's completely unintelligible. Supporting Leeds is a relationship; an experience that only those who engage in the deeply connective entanglement can truly make sense of even if, at times, it makes no sense at all and, in fact, has mostly felt downright painful for years now. That's the nature of some relationships. Why do we do it?

There's a whole world of research and theory that might go some way to explaining the 'why?' The effects of supporting a sports team is well documented in psychology; the Team Identification–Social Psychological Health Model hypothesis has consistently found positive relationships between sports team identification, social connections and psychological wellbeing. Studies have concluded that highly identified supporters have an above average sense of *meaning* in life.

You could factor in the 20% increase of feel-good testosterone levels when your team wins (in both supporters *and* players), you might add in Oxytocin, variously referred to as the Mother-Baby bonding, love or cuddle hormone, that's become increasingly identified as playing a vital role in trust and fidelity. Tip in dopamine – a pleasure/reward hormone which increases/decreases motivation and enthusiasm – and you've got a proper neuro-cocktail. The bottom line is there's a lot going on under the bonnet.

Now I'm no fan of rollercoaster rides, and maybe it's not the best metaphor anyway, but the reality is that when it comes to supporting Leeds, I've conclusively experienced a wild ride though physical, hormonal and emotional effects. Stuff that can be described by science, but also explained through the lens of a deep relational connection. From a psychotherapeutic perspective, we are relationship seeking creatures and make meaning through our relationships to people, objects and experiences. It's our relationships and own unique way of relating that creates our joy and pain. This is the stuff that I'm interested in as a counsellor and psychotherapist, both for my client's wellbeing and for my own too.

My emotional investment in Leeds feels huge, maybe not as big as I'm sure it does for some supporters, but it's my investment nonetheless. Why do I do it? Because it gives me something, a thing I pretty much find is beyond words; being with my 'football family' at ER, a weightlessness, a sense of sometimes having that voice, the collective voice as the twelfth man, that lifts the lads and urges them on, feeling (really FEELING) the joy of the win and those three points pushing us closer and closer. If we're lucky enough, there's some proper mind blowing experiences in life, but this is an experience unique to itself. But it's also a balancing act which can be cruel and downright feel-bad. What's certain is it's felt like I've been put through the wringer too much over the last sixteen years. The innumerable times I've felt utterly frustrated, deflated, miserable, angry, defeated... well, you know the feelings.

I know you might disagree but I've always pinpointed that Cardiff FA Cup match as some kind of bad juju tipping point. The Sam Hamman one. There just seemed to be some kind of tear in the fabric of the Leeds United space/time continuum after that match, a really slow motion pulling apart of the seam of our shared reality. From that moment it felt like a horrible, tainted emotional spiral gradually unfurling – as if our psyche was a skip being perpetually and unrelentingly filled with burning shit.

Bury your head in your hands as you flick through the Rolodex of LUFC despair.... sacking "O'Leary! O'Leary! O'Leary!", the fire sale, the agent's fees, El Tel, Peter 'it wasn't me' Ridsdale, Smudge's tears, your *own* tears...

'Are you actually crying? Because you've been relegated? REALLY?'

From bad to worse. That professor and a bloke from the post office, League One. LEAGUE ONE.

'15 points who gives a f***, we're super Leeds and we're going up', Dennis 'He was rubbish*' Wise (*© Robbie Blake), ropey sponsors (snifter of Whyte and McKay for your 2-stroke lawnmower mister?), Citizen Ken, administration, ticket prices going up ('It costs *HOW MUCH* to watch this shite????)

AND PAUSE.

Look, there were a couple of really good moments. Those two Beckford goals were manna and, for a bit of a light-hearted interlude of a SNAFU, Mad Friday, provided a bit of Sports TV bemused mirth. But let's face it, the rest of the time it was a chimpanzee scrawl on bog paper when you really wanted Rothko at the New York Museum of Modern Art. Onandonandonandon and unrelentingly on...The Colour Purple/Number 17/Women in football/Dave *WHO?* The Dante's inferno of mid-table purgatory, the fantasy island glimmer of hope with Monk. The pay-off? Beers, tears and the big screen Kop experience of shattered dreams...

'How much do you think you've spent supporting Leeds?'

'I don't even want to think about it...'

And yet...

And yet we never stopped believing did we? Well, maybe we did *occasionally* but we put the thought out of our minds sharpish because we always knew it would come good didn't we. *Didn't we?*

The fevered dreams...one day, one day, one day, one day, one day...

And then God arrived.

I'm not a religious man but when it comes to the idea of *this* living deity I'm willing to keep an open mind. If football can be considered a microcosm of life then it's quite possible that Bielsa is God. God with all his detailed creation, with his Plan A for us all, with his deific flaws. And God does get it wrong (Trump/sago/the workings of the PL), his leading us to the promised land was fatally ruptured right at the very end. The ecstasy and the agony. The misery of the play offs at home. That was really, really painful.

But with the foibles also comes the majestic brilliance. We went again and he gifted us, his children, with more. He gave us hope, poetry, beauty, kindness, awareness, he made the lads pick up litter. He gave us Arsenal in the FA Cup, Bielsa Ball, hammering Stoke and Boro, that mental Birmingham match, he showed us his weaknesses and his brilliance, he gave the lads murder ball.

He pushed us into an alternative reality, one in which the haters now told everyone how much they loved Leeds. God does indeed work in mysterious ways.

He gave us something unspoken, intangible; You and I know we never really lost our pride but over the last two seasons he gave us a thing we'd perhaps lost. A spark. The deep desire for the stuff that'd been going wrong in our relationship to go right. He exacted the things that weren't working, highlighted where we can change and, if it's possible, made us love Leeds even more. He gave us the tools to truly, madly, deeply love again.

We even loved Victor Orta, that's how much of a miracle worker he is. You're alright Victor, I got you wrong and I'm sorry mate. You stood at the foot of the mountain, you explained why we needed him to come down and he answered our prayers.

No matter how much we've spent (and let's face it, we'll never do the calculations), none of it matters now because, for however long the pain lasted, we are healed and we will always have last season.

'How much do you think you've spent supporting Leeds?'

'I've never worked it out but last season, finishing Campeones with a 12 point margin, was worth everything I've spent (pounds sterling and emotional).'

So not only is Bielsa God, he's also a very good therapeutic counsellor. I'm not a religious man but Praise Be for Bielsa Therapy.

Chris Madden —
Chris Madden MBACP is a counselling psychotherapist and Season Ticket Holder. First match 7 September 1974 Vs Luton Town.

Eric Cantona
LUFC
CENTENARY
CUP FINAL
1972

LUFC
F.A. CUP FINAL
1973

"Watching us become Champions of England in the 91/92 season was special looking back, but now for me it's not just the 90 minutes that matters, it's the full day or evening match experience with my family and friends. A good pint, win lose or draw with every visit to Elland Road a unique occasion in itself.

I've not really got a favourite item in my collection; it's like asking which is my favourite son. I love the lot but I have spells of appreciating some more than others for a while... At the moment, it's a gift that Marcelo gave me after our meetings up at Thorp Arch. (A signed 'To Ben' 2020/21 home shirt) I now have his signature tattooed on my arm, which he then told me he did not like. What a man, what a legend. We even discussed the ingredients of a chilli pork pie that I gave to him. He rang me just before the Liverpool game, to tell me it needed more chilli.

I'm seriously considering asking him to adopt me ha-ha!"

Ben Hunter
theleedsunitedcollection.co.uk

BATTY
BOWYER
T.ROBERTS
LUFC
FOSTERS
FAN ZONE
NOW OPEN AT HALFTIME
GET SERVED FASTER
Admiral

YEBOAH
21
32Red
Lisa Cooper
CAPTAIN
LEEDS UNITED AFC
Heads Up

Acknowledgements

Thank you

A big thank you to all the people who helped make this idea a reality.

Special thanks and love to my wife Jayne, Ashlea, Curtis, Adam, Mum & Bill, Katie Slee and Jodie Slee. Joey Barritt, Paul Carter, Andy Gray, Becky Palfery, Ryan Wilson, Liz Dimitrijevic, Matthew Bowman, Neil Jeffries, Hayden Evans, Colours May Vary, Doubletruck, The Leeds United Collection.

Marcelo Bielsa and all the managers, players and staff who have represented Leeds United Football Club.

To everyone who provided or assisted in contributing a quote included in the final print publication and to all the Leeds United supporters for the inspiration.

Credits

Concept & Photography
Justin Slee
justinslee.co.uk

Design
saul studio
saulstudio.co.uk

Print
Jump North
jumpdp.com

Quotes & Memories

David Batty, Matt Bowman, Aiden Butterworth, Liam Cooper, Danny Cullen, Stuart Dallas, Hayden Evans, Eddie Gray, Simon Grayson, Ian Harte, Phil Hay, Andrew Hughes, Ben Hunter, Ralph Ineson, Micky P Kerr, Bryn Law, Andy McVeigh (Burley Banksy), Lucas Radebe, Chaz Singh, Andrew Varley, Josh Warrington, Henry Winter.

Writers

Dave Best
Bass player in the platinum-selling Leeds band, The Pigeon Detectives. Also held a music and culture column in the *Yorkshire Evening Post*.

James Brown
Author of *Above Head Height* and creator of *Leeds Leeds Leeds* and *Loaded* magazines.

Robert Endeacott
Author of the Novels, *One Northern Soul, No More Heroes, Dirty Leeds, After Extra Time* and *The Gigante*.

Craig Ferguson
Craig Ferguson wrote regularly for *Leeds Leeds Leeds* magazine between 1997 and 2012 whilst working as a TV screenwriter.

Heidi Haigh
Curator of the blog, *Follow Me and Leeds United*, and Author of *Once a Leeds fan, always a Leeds fan* and *Leeds are going to the Premier League!*

Neil Jeffries
Editor of *Leeds Leeds Leeds* magazine for 13 years and also works on all things loud, with *Classic Rock Magazine* and all things Leeds, on the matchday programme.

Chris Madden
Chris Madden MBACP is a counselling psychotherapist and Season Ticket Holder. First match 7 September 1974 Vs Luton Town.

Ruth Saxton
Contributes to *The Square Ball* and works as a Community Producer for *Slung Low*.

Dave Simpson
Author of *The Last Champions – The Year That Football Changed Forever*, about the 1991/92 title season and onset of the Premiership.

"Of course, the trophy makes me happy, but I've worked in football for 30 years and one title doesn't change a lot to the percentage of trophies I have. What really makes me happy is the fact I did this project with this group of players across two years."

Marcelo Bielsa